T0067741

Kathy Whitworth's
Little Book of Golf Wisdom

ALSO BY KATHY WHITWORTH

Golf For Women:
Easy-to-follow Instruction from Pro Golf's
Leading Tournament Winner

Kathy Whitworth's Little Book of Golf Wisdom

A Lifetime of Lessons From Golf's Winningest Pro

———•◆•———

Kathy Whitworth
with Jay Golden, PGA

Skyhorse Publishing

Copyright © 2007 by Kathy Whitworth

All rights reserved. No part of this book may be reproduced in any manner without the express written consent of the publisher, except in the case of brief excerpts in critical reviews or articles. All inquiries should be addressed to Skyhorse Publishing, 307 West 36th Street, 11th Floor, New York, NY 10018.

Skyhorse Publishing books may be purchased in bulk at special discounts for sales promotion, corporate gifts, fund-raising, or educational purposes. Special editions can also be created to specifications. For details, contact the Special Sales Department, Skyhorse Publishing, 307 West 36th Street, 11th Floor, New York, NY 10018 or info@skyhorsepublishing.com.

Skyhorse® and Skyhorse Publishing® are registered trademarks of Skyhorse Publishing, Inc.®, a Delaware corporation.

Visit our website at www.skyhorsepublishing.com.

10 9 8 7 6 5 4 3 2 1

The Library of Congress cataloged the hardcover edition as follows:

    Whitworth, Kathy.
    Kathy Whitworth's little book of golf wisdom : a lifetime of
    lessons from golf winningest pro/Kathy Whitworth.
    p.cm.
    Includes bibliographical references and index.
    ISBN-13: 978-1-60239-022-5 (pbk. : alk. paper)
    ISBN-10: 1-60239-022-3 (pbk. : alk. paper)
    1.Whitworth, Kathy.2.Golfers—United States—
    Biography.3.Women golfers—United States—Anecdotes.
    4.Golf—Anecdotes.I.Title.

    GV964.W48W452007
    796.352092—dc22
    [B]
                      2006102478

Cover design by Eric Clark
Cover photo credit © Kay Bagwell, jacket art © Allposters.com

Paperback Print ISBN: 978-1-63220-655-8
Ebook ISBN 978-1-62636-796-8

Printed in China

I dedicate this book to all the wonderful people who helped me and encouraged me in any way; to those who developed the game; and to the pioneers who hit the first ball into the first hole. And finally, I dedicate this book to the game itself: Golf, the game that added so much meaning and happiness to my life.

TESTIMONIALS

The qualities that made Kathy the leading tournament winner of all time are reflected in this book. Her incredible career was fueled in part by her drive for perfection and her perceptiveness in understanding the game and all its nuances. This book gives golfers of all skill levels an opportunity to share in the amazing insights that Kathy reveals about golf. Kathy's perspective about the game, about the people with whom she played, and about her own successes and failures demonstrate clearly her warmth, her intelligence, and her great sense of humor. Her book epitomizes the Kathy Whitworth that I know—delightful in a hundred ways!

—BETSY RAWLS

Kathy Whitworth's success derives from her many admirable traits. Her multitude of wins is one of the great records in sports and certainly speaks of her competitive nature. Confidence in her innate feel, in her own swing and tempo combined with a beautiful and effective short game, served her in great stead in varying conditions. Harvey Penick thought the world of Kathy. I am certain that he taught her to believe in herself. Her cheerful demeanor belies a competitive toughness down the stretch.

These days Kathy enjoys teaching students what she knows about the game. Her knowledge as well as her many fine traits will benefit all golfers.

—BEN CRENSHAW

Eighty-eight! Can anyone ever imagine ever winning that many professional golf tournaments? This is more wins than any professional has ever amassed, male or female.

Just think for a moment. You play all the amateur golf you can find to try to get good enough to turn professional. You hit thousands and thousands of practice balls day after day just dreaming of competing against the likes of a Patty Berg, a Betsy Rawls or a Mickey Wright. Eventually after many defeats, along with a few wins, you learn how to control your emotions enough that the swing or the putting stroke does not waver too much when trying to hit that last drive in the fairway or sink that winning putt. Now, go ahead and do that for some 20 or 25 years. Win two or three tournaments EVERY year for 25 years and, you still find yourself way short of the record Kathy Whitworth set. This is such a high standard it is difficult to imagine anyone ever surpassing her record.

But as competitive as she has been throughout her long and illustrious career, there is no more caring person than Kathy. When Kathy's playing days were just about completed and she was thinking about teaching the game instead, she realized that playing at a high level was a long ways away from knowing how to communicate what to do in the golf swing. She sought advice from her long time teaching pro, Harvey Penick, who asked her if she played any musical instrument. After replying, "Of course not, I spend all my time playing golf," Harvey recommended she take a few lessons to learn how to play one. This obviously was not to give her any education on golf—she already knew all about that—but to teach her to have some empathy for the students she was about to teach. Those who excel at any endeavor often times have little patience when trying to describe how it is done to a novice. Kathy studied teaching golf the same way she learned how to play and has now gone on to become a top teacher, helping numerous golfers enjoy this great game.

Kathy's book also lives up to this high standard. Those of us that know her would not have expected anything less. Enjoy.

—TOM KITE

I have had the pleasure of knowing Kathy Whitworth for over 40 years and it's a privilege to call her a friend.

Isn't it fantastic that such a humble person has won more official tour events than any man or woman in the history of the game? I must tell you, achieving that accomplishment was no accident. It was the result of the combination of total dedication to excellence and clear, intelligent thinking.

When I was told that Kathy was writing a book in which a great extent was based on her thought processes, I was very interested. Winning takes so much more than just a good golf swing. As the great Ben Hogan said, "The answer is in the dirt!"

Whether it is golf course management, knowing your own game or how to handle pressure, the importance of the mental part of the game cannot be over-emphasized. Kathy excelled in these mental aspects and explains them brilliantly in this book.

It is intriguing how Kathy writes about learning from her "beautiful mistakes." So many golfers either ignore or make excuses for their bad shots. Kathy always searched for the reason why a shot didn't come off as she had planned. Isn't that a great attitude?

Another point that comes through loud and clear several times in this book is near and dear to my heart. That point is, "Never give up!" Kathy explains that if you don't give up and keep trying when your game is off, not only can you save a bad round but when your game is on, that quality makes good rounds even better. Never giving up proved itself to be true hundreds of times in my own career.

It's so interesting to find out how hard she tried. Kathy became one with the game as much as any player in history ever did. I laughed when I read that she not only thought about golf all day but that when she was sleeping and dreamt about a swing change, she would jump out of bed to see what it looked like in the mirror.

I admire Kathy for her perseverance, enthusiasm, commitment and for dedicating her life to this great game. I am also proud of her to be able to describe her thoughts and experiences in a way that can be easily understood and that can greatly benefit all those who read this excellent book.

—GARY PLAYER

When I came out on the LPGA Tour I already knew who Kathy Whitworth was. I played golf with her mom and her aunt when I played in the New Mexico Women's State Championship. They were very nice ladies. Since I was so young as an amateur, lots of the older women did not want me to play in their championship. Kathy's mom and aunt were great.

When I was about eleven or twelve Kathy and Carol Mann came to Roswell to do a clinic for our community. That's when I got to see Kathy hit a golf ball for the first time. She was very interesting to watch and was very kind to everyone.

When I got to the LPGA Tour she was just the same. Even though I was very young she treated me with great respect and made me feel welcomed. I played with her many times and she was a great shot maker and competitor. She was also just a great sport.

She was my captain on the first Solheim Cup played back in 1990. She was very calm and very professional throughout, and I was very glad she was my captain. We won that event and I got to know her a little more as a person, not just as a competitor. She is someone that is high on my list of people that I am glad to have known.

I appreciate everything she did for the LPGA Tour. She, of course, made it a better place for me when I came out on the tour. I will always wish her the best in life.

—NANCY LOPEZ KNIGHT

It's hard to believe I've known Kathy for almost 50 years. She is really special in many ways. She is determined, loyal to friends and to the LPGA, extremely hard working, and through all of her success in golf she has maintained a charming modesty. To call her the First Lady of the LPGA is not a stretch.

I feel honored to call her a friend.

—MICKEY WRIGHT

Contents

Introduction

IN 1958, a homespun nineteen-year-old girl from New Mexico named Kathy Whitworth took off in the family automobile with her mother to embark on a career on the LPGA Tour. By the time she returned home at the age of fifty, she had won more official tour events than any golfer in the history of the game.

Having known Kathy personally and professionally, I was confident that if she shared her process in a book, it would help golfers achieve their goals by giving them her unique perspective.

As this project moved along, I realized that it was much more profound, philosophical and insightful than I had ever imagined. Kathy's self analysis, dedication, and knowledge were something to behold. She is a shrewd, perceptive, and intuitive woman.

After every round throughout her career, Kathy would take note of her physical and mental mistakes. Whereas many people defend and rationalize their mistakes, Kathy welcomed mistakes and viewed them as "beautiful." She felt that if she was able to identify her mistakes, it gave her the opportunity to fix them and not repeat them. This was one of Kathy's greatest strengths as a golfer. Whether the mistake was mental or physical, she had a keen sense of self awareness for even the slightest mishap. And as Kathy said, "Sometimes the tough part is noticing it."

As a golfer, Kathy was the combination of a brilliant detective finding clues, a scientist objectively searching for answers, and Will Rogers, who always kept it simple for plain folk.

Believe me, the first person to disagree with those comparisons would be the humble Kathy Whitworth.

In reading this book, you will find out what worked and what didn't work for the most prolific winner of all time, along with many heart-warming stories. And whether you follow down her path to success or are inspired to blaze new trails of your own, Kathy's priceless thoughts and experiences are sure to guide you along the way.

—Jay Golden
December, 2006

Do You Want
to be #1?

PERHAPS YOU'D LIKE to be the #1 player in the world, #1 at your club, shoot your #1 lowest score, hit your #1 best shot ever, or be the #1 best that you could be.

By the way, being the #1 best you could be is probably the greatest #1.

If you want to be #1, I hope there are things in this book that will help.

Here's a bit of an overview of this book and what it takes to be #1.

* * * * *

First and most importantly, you have to enjoy what you're doing. If you don't enjoy the process, or if you're doing it for someone else, it's probably not going to work.

Next is to break the game down into its essential parts. You have to work on your entire game and that starts with improving your swing. I was lucky to have a great teacher, Harvey Penick. It would be a good idea if you could find a good teacher too.

When you make a mistake, figure out why and try not to make it again. Be honest with yourself. I always felt that every bad shot was my fault. Learn how to never give up and keep trying. Play through nervousness.

Learn how to manage a course. That starts with hitting away from trouble and playing your most consistent shot.

You have to break scoring back down to its essentials. Play one shot at a time. Get good at every shot. That comes from learning their fundamentals and practicing what you've learned. Winning is the goal, but it really does take care of itself by playing well.

The attitude that "I could always do better" is important. It was for me. A reporter interviewing me after shooting a 70 made the comment that I didn't seem happy. I said, "If you're satisfied with a 70, you're never going to shoot 69." Always try to improve. Always keep trying to get better.

Becoming #1 takes a lot of work and knowing the right things to do.

Good luck. If you try hard enough, you can do it.

Trusting a Teacher

WHATEVER SPORT YOU play, you have to have help to succeed. When you look at the best players, they all had really good instructors while they were going through the process. You need someone who can put the fundamentals in place. Then, of course, what you do with them is up to you.

I don't care how much natural ability a person has. You have to learn the fundamentals, and it's so difficult to learn them by yourself. It's important to have a teacher who knows them and can explain them in a way that is easy to understand.

Another reason why a good teacher is important is that you could be playing well for a while and then your game starts deteriorating. It's usually because one of the fundamentals has gone off. That's when you need somebody who knows your swing and who you can trust. Every time I got into a slump or started hitting the ball poorly, I had Harvey Penick to go to. Harvey would usually pick out the mistake right away and it was almost always a fundamental that I wasn't doing correctly.

One time in particular, and I don't know why, the clubface was open at address. As a result, I couldn't line up. Then I was either snap hooking because I was overcompensating or hitting it to the right because that's where the clubface was aiming. It was all due to the clubface not being square at address.

I went to Harvey and after about 10 shots he knew what it was. Then by squaring the clubface at address, everything fell back into place. I couldn't see the mistake myself and there probably weren't very many people who would have picked that out because they didn't know my swing. Harvey knew the fundamentals and he knew my swing.

Harvey saw that it was an open clubface and then showed it to me by stepping into my stance. There was a confidence factor. He was just the best. I don't know how else to say it except that I was very lucky and fortunate to have that kind of instruction.

For me, the first element to playing well was good instruction. If you want to improve, get that information somewhere. Look at Tiger. He's always trying to get better. I'm sure he has a great understanding of his swing and certainly has good fundamentals, but he always goes for help.

You can't do it on your own. I had Harvey. He was a marvelous teacher and was someone I could trust.

Get Good at Every Shot

YOU NEED TO be able to hit all the shots. There aren't too many winners who can't play them all. Some might be a little better at certain aspects of the game, but they're all pretty good at hitting every shot when they need it.

There are so many shots that are needed in a round of golf. Shots fall into general categories like drives, irons, pitches, chips, sand shots, trouble shots, and putts, but there are variations within each of these categories.

You might need draws, fades, slices, hooks, high shots, and low ones. And what really multiplies the number is to be able to hit these shots from sidehill lies, as well as the different lies you can get in the fairway and the rough. Winners know how to hit all of these shots. You can see that with Tiger Woods. Whatever the situation, he has a shot for it and more times than not he hits a good one.

If you want to shoot low scores consistently, to be in contention and to win, get good at every shot. That's what I tried to do and I enjoyed every minute of it.

Think of the Target

I couldn't think about my swing on the golf course. I tried it but it didn't work. There were even times when I'd give myself lessons on the course. OUCH! The main reason it didn't work was that I didn't know where the target was. While I was swinging, I didn't have an awareness of where I wanted to hit the ball.

When you're standing on the first tee, the round is on and you don't have a second chance. It's not the driving range. You have to trust your swing. If you're thinking about your swing, do you really trust it? Also, you forget about where you're trying to hit the ball. There are so many things that you need to be thinking about and your swing is the last one. I had to quit doing that.

Thinking about my swing instead of thinking about the target led to uncertainty. In fact, it eventually resulted in paralysis by analysis. That's what practice was all about.

I worked on my swing on the range. When I was on the course, I thought about the target.

When you're on the course, you've got to put your swing in play. You have to trust it. Think about the target and go.

It was tough, but I had to make myself do it. I told myself that I can't play the other way so I might as well let it rip at the target. Then wherever it goes it goes.

Harvey said, "The greatest pressure reliever in golf is to think about the target."

I really started to play when I stopped thinking about the swing and started thinking about the target. If you don't know where you're going, there's less of a chance that you'll get there.

I Always Tried to Get Better

I DON'T KNOW where it came from. Maybe it came from my parents. They always worked hard. They didn't go to college, but they were extremely smart. They always tried to do the best they could. Dad eventually opened a hardware store and was always trying to make the store better.

Mom had many projects. She worked in the store and was involved in organizations. She was very good at charity work and did a lot of that.

Whatever I was interested in, I tried to do the best I could. The most fun I ever had was being in the high school band.

I was the bass drummer. My oldest sister was a drummer and I wanted to be like her. I wasn't a great drummer, but I was the biggest kid in the school and I could carry it.

Not that I wanted to be the best drummer ever, it's just that I enjoyed it so much and tried to get better. I remember my older sister Carlynne going up to Eastern University. They had a big parade and they invited all the local bands to come up and march. So we went up there to march. I was learning how to twirl my sticks.

I wasn't aware of it at the time, but as it turned out I was doing my twirling thing and afterwards Carlynne made the comment, "Oh, you made quite a splash out there." I said, "What are you talking about?" She said, "Everyone was talking about the kid from Jal, New Mexico, just twirling those sticks!"

I didn't do it to show off. It was just so much fun to do. I saw someone else do it and I thought maybe I could, too. I also painted a panther on the drum to make it look sharp. The motivation was that I just wanted to be better. It wasn't that I was trying to beat anybody. There was nobody there to beat except the drum.

In every sport that I played, I tried to improve. It was fun. Dad put up a basketball goal in the backyard and I'd take shot after shot. When I started playing tennis, I would practice hitting the ball against a brick wall for hours.

But I remember clearly that when I was a kid I wasn't trying to beat anybody. I just wanted to be better. I admired other people's ability and then I'd ask myself, "If they can do it, why can't I?"

Once in a post-round interview after shooting a 70, a reporter commented that I didn't seem satisfied. Although 70 was a good score, the reporter was right. I wasn't satisfied because there were shots that didn't come off as I hoped and I knew that I could do better.

If I wanted to shoot low scores consistently, I knew that I had to improve. That's true in any craft or field. To improve, it all boils down to effort.

I went on to say to the reporter, "If you're satisfied with a 70, you'll never shoot a 69!" I realize that statement isn't totally true, but I said it because I used it as a personal reminder.

Trying was the operative word. I kept trying to improve all aspects of my game. That's the only way you'll ever know how good you can get. You have to know in your heart that you are trying your best.

Finding a Teacher

I WAS LUCKY that my first teacher, Hardy Loudermilk, had the insight to send me to Harvey Penick when I got to a certain level. I shudder to think what my career might have been if I didn't meet Hardy and Harvey.

I really don't know how you can find a knowledgeable teacher who you'll like and trust, but here are a few ideas. Go to a few teachers at nearby golf courses and driving ranges to see if there's someone you can relate to. Ask some of the better golfers in your area who they take lessons from. Find out who is the LPGA or PGA Teacher of the Year in your local section.

If you respect a teacher, that's important. If a teacher I didn't know told me certain things, I might not have listened to that person even though they may have been right. I needed to respect the teacher first.

Early on, Harvey told me in a kind but firm way, "I think I can help you, but you have to do what I say. If you don't, you'll be wasting your time and mine." I just said "Yes sir." If he told me to stand on my head, I would have stood on my head. That's not to say that Harvey didn't ask me questions to get my input, because he did. That was just our mindset going in.

But Harvey wasn't for everybody. He said that himself. There were a lot of pros that came to him and didn't stick with him. I know one pro who went to him and said, "I love Harvey, but he just isn't for me." She needed a different kind of teacher.

I just don't know the answer as to how to find a teacher. Find someone you can relate to. If you take a few lessons and you're still not happy, go elsewhere. Sometimes it's just a matter of communication. You just might not like the way they present the information. That's okay. Go somewhere else. You're not locked into that individual. Even tour pros hop around looking for the right teacher.

In some ways it's a crapshoot. Remember, not every pro is for every person. I was lucky that Harvey was right for me.

One Shot at a Time

ONCE I HAD a good golf game, one of the most important ingredients to playing well consistently was learning to focus on playing one shot at a time.

You don't have control over a shot that you've already played or a shot you'll play later, just the shot that you're playing. That's why I always gave it my complete attention.

It sounds easy, but it takes a lot of discipline. The way I developed that discipline was to make it a priority. Before teeing off, I made it a goal to think clearly about each individual shot. That meant checking the lie, the distance, the wind, the firmness of the ground, the shot that was needed, the bail out area, and my most reliable shot from that position. Then I did my pre-shot routine and thought about the target while swinging. I made it a priority to do that on every shot.

You might be wondering why it's hard to do that on every shot. It's hard because you might not be thinking clearly. For example, it's easier to think clearly on a tee shot after making a solid par on a difficult hole than it is after making a double bogey on a short par five. I'm sure you know what I mean.

After a bad hole nobody could possibly have been unhappier than me. But I learned through experience that if I focused on a previous bad shot, I'd likely make mistakes on the next hole. I'd start bogeying two or three holes in a row. Finally, I said to myself, "I can't afford to do that. Just because I messed up one hole, that doesn't mean I have to mess up the next one and maybe the one after that!"

If you clear your mind and try your best on each shot, it becomes a habit and it's a great habit to get into. Betsy Rawls said, "I work harder for an 80 than I do for a 70." When you are playing badly, it's hard to keep your mind clear and to play one shot at a time. But you have to. An 80 is better than an 81. It's something that you have to make yourself do. It's not something that you're born with. You have to learn it.

I made it a priority to give it my all on each individual shot. I concentrated on one shot at a time, as if each was the first shot of the day. There's no doubt that it helped me a lot. I guess that you could say that it became a habit, but it was a great habit to get into.

It seems like every time the winner of a tournament is interviewed they say, "Today I was able to play one shot at a time."

My First Three Days
with Harvey

THE FIRST TIME that I went to see Harvey, Mom and I drove 500 miles to Austin and we spent three days there. Believe it or not, all we worked on was the grip and a square clubface at address. That doesn't sound like much, but placing your hands on the grip with a square clubface sets up everything in the swing.

Before seeing Harvey, I'm sure I was doing the same thing that everyone else did. Keep the left arm straight and all that stuff. Harvey said to put my hands on the club and to be sure the face was square. I'd do it and he'd ask me to take my hands off and start over. I did that over and over again.

To get the clubface square I had to place my hands on the club without twisting them because that would cause tension in the elbows and shoulders. The result was that the clubface would turn. It was just placing my hands on the club that Harvey wanted.

Once I got them on the club, he asked me to squeeze the grip just enough to set the club on the ground. That was the grip pressure he wanted, just enough to feel the weight of the club as I set it on the ground. By squeezing it a bit, I could see if the clubface toed in or opened up as I set it on the ground. If it did, I'd have to start over.

The reason a square clubface is so important is that if it isn't square, you'll need to make some adjustment in your swing. It becomes a matter of compensations.

For example, if the ball is going low and left due to a closed clubface at address, you might try to solve that by hanging on a little longer with the left hand. Then the ball might start going to the right. But all of that happens because there is a closed clubface at address. You are just trying to make an adjustment. If you start with a square blade, a lot of problems just go away.

I finally got my hands on the club and took a swing. I thought that I was doing pretty well and he'd say, "You changed your grip during the swing." I was just mortified.

"The next time, when you finish your swing," Harvey said, "Take your club and put it back at address." Sure enough, I did it and the face was shut. It was a bad habit and I had to change.

I have to tell you, the best thing in the world he ever taught me was my grip and a square clubface. All through my career, I knew that if something went wrong with my swing, the first thing to check was my grip and the clubface. More times than not, it was the source of my problem.

Know Your Strengths

IN A PERFECT WORLD, you'll always know what shot is called for depending on the pin position, the layout of the hole, and other factors. The perfect shot might be a high fade, a low draw, or whatever. You'd know the shot that should be played if you had every shot in the bag, but can you hit every shot with consistency? Most people can't.

If the pin is on the front left side of the green, it calls for a high, soft draw. But is a high draw your highest percentage shot? You must also take into consideration how you're playing at the time. Are you on top of your game? If not, what are the chances that you'll pull that shot off? Those are the factors to take into consideration and you have to come to an honest answer.

My best shot was a fade. Off the tee I could usually control it, and I had the confidence that I could get the ball in the fairway. It might have not looked very pretty, but it was effective. Fortunately there's no room on the scorecard for pictures. If I hit my fade, at least I knew that I wasn't going to beat myself.

If I was playing well and had confidence, I played almost all of the shots. But in general, I played to my strengths. That goes back to having control over your swing and control over your thinking. Then it's knowing your highest percentage shot at that moment and choosing that shot to hit.

Mickey Wright could hit a high draw with a 2-iron that looked like it was shot out of a cannon. For me to try to hit that shot, and hit it like Mickey, would have been a mistake, so I didn't try it. I'd play a shot that was easier for me. I might play my bread and butter fade with a 3-wood. In that situation I wouldn't try to hit the perfect shot. I played my highest-percentage shot.

We all have our strengths and we have to know what they are so we can choose the shot that we can best execute.

Bring Your Driving Range Swing to the Course

THE FIRST STEP to bringing your driving-range swing to the golf course is to bring your golf-course swing to the driving range. In other words, you have to be more serious when you hit balls on the range, and do the same things on the range that you do on the course.

I hear this from golfers all the time. "I hit the ball great on the practice tee but I didn't hit it a lick on the course." The main reason this happens is that on the practice tee they weren't thinking the same or doing the same things that they did on the course.

On the range they were swinging freely to a wide open field, knowing that there's always another ball to hit if they hit a bad one. There was no pressure, they felt loose and bam, bam, bam. They hit it great. On the practice tee, they were just whaling away, but that's not what they did on the course.

Now they're on the first tee. They only have one ball and they want to hit it on the fairway. They aim and they feel a little tighter. It's a different ball game. They're aiming on the course and their driving range swing goes out the window.

Harvey would never let me hit a shot, even on the range, without aiming. The first step was to pick a target and then "take dead aim." He felt that if you were practicing without aiming you were wasting your time. Harvey would say, "don't let all this practice go to waste. Make it count. Hit to a target."

Even if you're working on your swing on the range and thinking about this or that, you should be aiming, and your last thought should still be hitting the ball at the target. Most golfers focus only on their swing with no target awareness, and that's why they lose their driving-range swing when they get on the course.

During one of my early sessions with Harvey, he said that he had to go to the clubhouse to do something. Before leaving he made the point, "Aim and concentrate on the target. Don't just hit without aiming and thinking about the target." I said, "Okay."

I guess he knew to point that out to me because as soon as he left, I hit without aiming or thinking where I wanted to hit the ball. I just hit them bam, bam, bam, without concentrating.

When he came back he said, "Now let's see you hit a good one for me." This time I aimed, thought about the target and hit a bad shot. Point well taken! Once again Harvey was right. If I had been practicing as he suggested, I would have hit a better shot.

15

To have a better chance of hitting a good shot on the course, practice the way you play. Bring your golf-course swing to the driving range and you'll bring your driving-range swing to the course.

To Play or to Practice?

EVERYONE IS DIFFERENT. Some players love to practice and others love to play. Two of Harvey's students, Ben Crenshaw and Tom Kite, fell into each of those categories. Harvey would say that he tried his best to get Tom off the practice tee and on the course and to get Ben off the course on the practice tee.

I practiced because I felt that I needed to, but really, I preferred playing. I felt that if I wanted to get better, I had to hit balls.

Just not hit balls, but to spend time on all aspects of the game. There are some players who pound balls all of the time and think that they are doing the right thing. Actually they're not. Players who just beat balls and don't work on their short game usually don't develop into very good players.

When I first started, I practiced for hours. I practiced before I teed off and after I got in. I had to practice a lot early on. I would work on my weaknesses more that my strengths.

That's not to say that you shouldn't spend time on the course. You have to learn how to get the ball in the hole. After all, that's the objective of the game. The only place you can learn that is playing on the course, and playing in competition is even better.

What is the correct amount of time to spend on each? I'd say about half the time playing and the other half practicing.

Snap Out of It!

———•◦•———

ALTHOUGH IT DOESN'T look very good, I don't really mind if a player gets upset after a bad shot or a bad hole. Of course, that's as long as they regain their composure by the time they hit their next shot.

Tiger Woods is probably the best example of getting upset, but then regaining his composure. It irritates him so much when he makes a mistake. But he doesn't allow it to affect his next shot. He just keeps trying, and that's one of his greatest qualities. He might be chipping for a double bogey, but he's trying as hard as he can to sink it.

If you don't learn how to "Snap out of it," you're in for a long day on the course and a short stay on the tour.

Know Your Weaknesses

———•◦•———

SOMETIMES MY WEAKNESSES were obvious. When I first went on tour it was clear to me that I was a bad putter. I didn't have to be a genius to realize that, and I knew I had to improve in that area.

I also knew that I was a terrible trap player. The worst example of this happened in my rookie year. I was the leader after the first round and it was the first time that I had led a tour event. I was paired with the great Patty Berg.

On a par three on the front nine, I hit my tee shot over the green into the back bunker. Then I shanked my sand shot into the right bunker and proceeded to skull the next bunker shot out-of-bounds. It was just awful. Let's just say that I didn't birdie the hole. That stuck with me big time, and I learned from it.

Other times my weaknesses were less obvious to me until I observed the other players. I was fortunate to be able to play with the best players on the LPGA Tour early in my career. I'd watch them very carefully in terms of the shots they'd play and how successful they were. If they had a shot that was consistently better than mine, I'd say to myself, "If they could hit it, why can't I?" I felt that with learning and practice I could hit the shots that the other players did.

The first step, however, was to have my eyes wide open, to be honest with myself, and to recognize my weaknesses.

Good Misses

YOU GET TO a certain level of proficiency in professional golf. Your swing is pretty good and your misses still pretty much go where you want them to. Maybe it's a little on the toe or heel, or you hit it a little left or right, but you're still not in trouble. You're still on the green. You're still on the fairway.

I'd miss a shot and I'd say to myself, "Oh man, what the heck did I do on that swing?" Then someone would say, "Good shot!" It might look good to someone else, but I knew that I didn't hit it the way I wanted to. One thing was for sure, it wasn't good to me.

When you think about it, why did the other person say, "Good shot?" They said it because the ball was hit in the right direction and ended up in a good place. That really is the purpose, isn't it?

A personal dream might be to hit every shot perfectly, but a good miss is one of the best shots in golf.

Target Practice

PRACTICE IS ALL about repeating something so it becomes automatic when you're on the course. A great place to practice thinking about the target is on the range.

Harvey would always say "Take dead aim" every time you hit a golf shot. Whether you're on the driving range or on the course, always "Take dead aim."

He never wanted any of his students to just hit balls without knowing where they were aiming, because that was never the situation when they were playing. On the course, you're always aiming at a target.

He always felt that when you practice, it should be as close as possible to what you do when you're playing. Just hitting into an open field without aiming wasn't something that you did when you played, so why would you do it when you practice? So many times I'll see golfers just hitting balls. Sometimes I'll ask them, "Where are you aiming?" They'll say, "I don't know. I'm just hitting."

To get the gist of it, do your pre-shot routine and "Take dead aim." During your swing, only think about the target. Don't give in to the temptation of thinking about positions or moves. Only think about where you want to hit the ball.

Controlling Your Distances

———◦•◦———

DISTANCE CONTROL IS one of the key factors for approach shots to the green. It doesn't matter what club you're hitting, you must be able to control the distance of the shot. If you know your game and how far you carry the ball, it's a major advantage.

I played my 5 iron to carry 150 yards. It might carry 155 or 145 but I was going to be within 5 yards of where I wanted it. Sometimes, depending on the lie or the conditions, I would control the speed of the club coming through the hitting area to hit it softer or harder. But you have to know how far you can depend on hitting the ball. You may not always execute the shot correctly, but you have to know that you can hit a shot or a club a certain distance.

Keep in mind that you should also be able to control the distance on pitch shots. I always get amused when an announcer says that a player lays up to a certain yardage so they can hit a full shot. That acknowledges there are some shots where they lack confidence in controlling their distance.

Whether it's full shots, part shots, type shots, wedges, chips, sand shots, or putting, you have to control your distances to play your best golf.

Pre-Shot Routine

MY PRE-SHOT ROUTINE was seeing the line from behind the ball, taking my grip while looking at the clubface, setting the club-head behind the ball, aiming the clubface at the target, squaring my body to the clubface, and stepping my left foot to the left and my right foot to the right. The distance that I stepped with each foot depended on which club I was hitting.

The pre-shot routine was the bedrock fundamental of my golf game.

The Ultimate Goal

WHAT WE'RE ALL trying to do is to square the clubface at impact while swinging down the line. That's what directs the shot and the correct combination of clubface and path will hit a straight shot every time.

Of course it's very hard to do, but if you keep trying, it will give you a reference when you want to swing a little inside-out or outside-in to hit draws and fades.

It sure would be great if we could synchronize swinging down the line with the clubhead facing the target at impact.

Good luck!

Rookie Paranoia

I WAS SO SELF-CONSCIOUS. I thought that everyone was looking at me. I guess I was also afraid. My mind would go off in crazy directions. I'd think, "What if I whiff it?"

That's just lack of confidence and not enough tournament exposure. Part of it was feeling that every eye in the world was on me, but that was so far from the truth.

Once I realized that everyone was concerned with their own game and not mine, it helped a lot. Also, when I understood that I would live through it and it wasn't the end of the world, that also calmed me down quite a bit.

The Quickest Way to Learn

THE QUICKEST WAY to learn something is to keep doing it over and over. That might sound like the long way but, compared to experimenting with this and that, it's the shortest road.

In my very first session with Harvey, he wanted me to take my grip while looking at the clubface to make sure it was square. It was "hands on, check the clubface, hands off. Start over." I did that time after time. Believe it or not, I spent three days with him during my first visit and that was basically all we did!

Although I didn't get that down perfectly, I achieved a level of success that could have taken a year or more if I had worked on it only once in a while. That's if I ever would have gotten it at all.

Try this the next time you go to the range. After every shot, take your hands off the club, put your hands on, and square the clubface. That's hands off, hands on, square the clubface, hit, and start over. By the end of this session, I dare you to say that the clubface isn't square at address. You won't be able to do it any other way.

Golfers love to experiment, jumping from one thing to the next and most of the time don't end up where they had hoped to. If you know that something is right, do it over and over again. It's the quickest way to learn.

Keep Grinding

PEOPLE CALL IT different things ranging from emotional control, concentration, focus or being in the zone. There's all kinds of terminology for the same thing, but it all boils down to "Keep Grinding."

It's a mindset. Tiger Woods made a comment after shooting 79 in the British Open one year, and I just love it. He said something like, "The way I was playing I couldn't have shot one stroke less. I tried my hardest on every shot. If I hadn't been trying my hardest, I would have shot worse." I just thought, "Good for you." He was grinding as much as he could and doing the best he could under the circumstances. He wasn't giving up on any shot. That mindset is just wonderful.

That's what I learned from the better players when I first went out on tour. When they weren't striking the ball as well as they could, or were struggling, they never gave up on any shot. I once saw Betsy Rawls get it up and down off the side of a mountain and save par. She wasn't bemoaning the fact that she hit it up there. Instead, she was thinking "What shot could I play to get the ball back into position?" It's exactly that kind of mental toughness that you have to develop to succeed at golf.

It's a discipline. It's not just something that you just turn on and off. It's a great habit if you can get into it. Keep grinding!

Not all Down and Ups are Easy

I WAS SITTING on the dais at a golf dinner one night and it was my turn to speak. I was introduced and that's when I realized that not all down and ups are easy.

I had on a long dress and when I sat down I accidentally put the chair legs on the bottom of my dress. I tried to get up but I couldn't. I was stuck and I almost fell backwards. It's just one of those times when you want to be perfect, and you almost fall off the dais backwards.

You look and feel horrified, but you just have to laugh. I was so embarrassed, but it's actually funny when those things happen.

For some reason Harvey never taught me how get down and up with chair legs on my dress.

I forgave him.

Golf Shot Management

PICKING THE SHOT that gave me my best chance for success was a huge part of playing my best golf. It boiled down to choosing the shot that came easiest to me. That dictated my choice. You have to learn what your best shot is under different circumstances and then choose that shot and hit it.

Some people might want to hit a low hook in a wind situation. I might want to hit a high fade because that is my better shot, even though it may not be the perfect shot for that situation. But it was the perfect shot for me because I could pull it off. If that's my best shot and the lie allows me to hit it, it's the shot that I should hit.

Take an honest look at your strengths. The shot that gives you your best chance for success is the shot that you should play.

Working the Ball

IN GENERAL, WHEN I hit a fade, I'd get a little quicker with my arms on the downswing, and for a draw I'd slow them down. The more you want to hook it, the more slowly you go through the hitting area to make sure that the face shuts down. Quicker arms are important on a fade, so there's less time for the clubface to turn over and it could be slightly open at impact.

To keep the ball low, the first thing I would do was to take more club. If I had a short iron to the green, let's say an 8-iron, I would take two clubs more and go to a 6-iron. I'd move the ball about an inch farther back in my stance. I'd make sure that I brought the club back low and that I kept it low coming through the ball. I'd stop my follow through about waist high. I'd do the same things for middle and long irons except that I'd only take one more club.

Clubhead awareness is vital when working the ball because the path of the club, and where the clubhead is facing at impact, determines everything.

How I Worked the Ball

WORKING THE BALL was a big advantage for me. It allowed me to adapt my game to different courses and weather conditions. In fact, it was probably the main reason I was able to be in contention as often as I was.

If you work the ball, there's more room for error because you can aim for the fat part of the green and work the ball towards the hole. The advantage was that if I hit a less-than-perfect shot, most of the time my miss would still be on the dance floor. Also, there weren't too many pins that I couldn't get to. I was always trying to work the ball somehow.

Working the ball was also an advantage in the wind. By keeping it low, hitting draws into fade winds, riding the wind, and hitting other type shots, I was able to keep my ball in play.

Working the ball for trouble shots was a prerequisite. Whether it was a big slice or a big hook, a high or low shot, or combinations of them, I needed to work the ball from trouble.

Also, hitting all of those shots and seeing which ones worked best and came easiest to me led me to find the fade, which I chose as my go-to shot.

I never won a tournament until I played a fade and I never knew how to hit a fade until I learned how to work the ball.

Four Types of Slices

WHEN I WANTED to move the ball left to right, I had four shots that curved different amounts.

The biggest curve was the slice. I didn't use a slice very much unless I was in trouble and needed to curve the ball quite a bit from behind a tree. I hit a slice by opening the clubface at address and cutting across the line, outside-in.

A fade curved less than a slice, but in a way was a small slice. I opened the clubface a hair at address and swung a tiny bit outside-in. The ball started a little to the left and curved back to the right.

On my cut shot, instead of the ball starting to the left, it started straight where I was aiming. It flew straight until it got to its highest point and then fell to the right. To hit the cut, I started with a square clubface and held on a little at impact.

The block was not a pretty shot, but I knew where it was going. The ball would start to the right of where I was aiming and then it would fade. I hit that by holding on and not letting the clubface turn over at all. It felt like I was still holding on in my follow through. I just never let the club turn over.

Trust me, the block was not going left!

Draws and Hooks

———•◆•———

THE PRINCIPLE FOR a ball to curve right-to-left is for the clubhead to be facing to the left of the direction that it is traveling. In other words, if the path of the clubhead is to the right of the target and the clubhead is facing at the target, the ball will start to the right of the target and curve right-to-left. The more the clubhead faces to the left of where it's traveling, the more the ball will hook.

Usually a hook is the lower shot because you de-loft the club and fades go higher because the face is a little bit open at impact.

I Never Won Until I Hit a Fade

———•◆•———

WHEN I FIRST went on the tour, everyone wanted to hook the ball. I hit a big hook. Hitting a draw would have been okay but I couldn't hit a draw consistently. The main reason my hook was bad was that when I overcooked it, it became a duck hook. You can't recover from that.

They say you can talk to a fade but you can't talk to a hook. That's not completely true. When I hit a duck hook I would talk to it, though I can't repeat what I said.

There's no question that going to a fade was a big turnaround for me. I'm not sure exactly when I started to play the fade, but it was probably after I did the clinics with Patty. I had to learn to hit different shaped shots, and until then I didn't know how to hit a fade.

I could control a fade. It started a little left and curved softly to the right. But I couldn't control a hook. A hook was just a wild thing and got me into a lot of trouble. Even when I hit irons to the green, it was tough to control. Many times it would hit the green and roll off.

Another challenging thing about a hook is when the pressure is on, because your timing has to be perfect to square the clubface. You come into the ball with a snap and when you snap it too soon, you hit a big hook.

Another disadvantage of hitting a hook is when you need to hit a fade. Since the swing is on such a different path, it's difficult to pull off. To hit a hook, the clubhead goes inside-out, but to hit a fade you do the opposite. It wasn't easy swinging a little outside-in across the line when all of my other swings were inside-out.

I needed to know how to hook when the situation called for it, but I never played really well until I stopped hitting a hook and started playing a fade. I hit my drives a little shorter and I needed one more club hitting irons into the greens, because it's a softer ball flight with more backspin.

It wasn't until I learned how to fade the ball that I was able to play consistently. I never won until I played a fade.

Aim Away from Trouble

My strategy was always to aim away from trouble. If I was hitting a tee shot and there was a lake, out-of-bounds, or fairway bunkers to the right side of the fairway, I would tee it up on the right side and hit away from the trouble by aiming down the left side of the fairway. If the trouble was on the left, I would do the opposite and tee up on the left side of the tee and hit away from it by aiming down the right side.

Depending on how well I was playing, the wind conditions, the firmness and slope of the fairway, I might play a fade or a draw. But one thing was for sure, I wasn't going to flirt with trouble.

See where the trouble is and stay away from it.

That's not a bad mindset for off the course as well.

Pull the Trigger

EARLY IN MY career there were times when doubt crept into my mind as I stood over the ball. It was usually because I was wondering if my swing was going to work. There was one thing that I found out for sure. Wondering led to being tentative and uncommitted and that didn't work.

When I was standing over a shot, I wanted to be in a position where I had confidence in my swing and all I had to do was to pull the trigger.

Realizing that last-second doubts were bad, I made sure to choose a shot that I could hit. I picked a shot that I had confidence in. Next I went through my pre-shot routine, thought about the target, and just pulled the trigger. As a result, I swung the club with confidence. I may not have always hit the exact shot that I wanted, but I was always committed to it.

My First Lead

THE FIRST TOURNAMENT that I led on the LPGA Tour was in my rookie year. I wasn't afraid being in the lead, but I didn't know how to act. I tried to act the way I thought everyone else acted. I said to myself, "Oh, this isn't important. I'll just play like it's a walk in the park." Of course I didn't feel that way very long. I think you know where I'm going.

That's right. I lost the lead quite quickly in the second round while paired with Patty Berg. I shot an 80. It was 44-36. I took some consolation in the fact that I brought it back on the second nine.

But it was a learning experience. As my career moved on, I eventually got to the point where I said to myself that it was okay to be nervous and it was acceptable not knowing what to do or how to handle it. I tried to be realistic and honest with myself.

I just laugh every time I think about that second round. It was just so much fun. I could hardly sleep a wink the night before. All night I was thinking, "I'm leading the tournament after the first round. Yippee!"

Listening and Watching

I WOULD TRY to listen when the best players were talking amongst themselves. Since the fields were smaller then, I was around all of these great players all the time. I listened to Betsy Rawls, Mickey Wright, Louise Suggs, Patty Berg, and Betty Jamison.

31

There were so many of them. It was great. They talked about shots they played or the round they had. They'd say, "Let me tell you about what I did on this hole." I was all ears and would pick up a lot of things that way.

I also loved watching them play. I learned so much just by observing. Even when I wasn't playing all that well, because of the size of the field, there were times when I'd still get paired with them and it was always a learning experience.

Observing the good and bad traits of the pros that I was playing with was always important to me. I watched how they conducted themselves, their club selection, shot selection, everything.

If you're open to it, you could always learn something by listening and watching.

Be Careful Who You Listen To

HARVEY TOLD ME, if I needed help, to "be careful who you listen to. Nine times out of ten they are going to tell you what they are working on. It won't relate to anything that you need to help you with your swing."

I followed his advice and almost never asked a player for help. It wasn't that I thought that they couldn't help me, but what he said turned me off. The exception was asking Mickey Wright an occasional question.

If I was having problems with my swing, Harvey gave me a checklist of things to go through myself, which worked out quite well.

Putting Practice

I FELT THAT if I practiced putting a lot I'd develop a fairly decent stroke, but I never spent a lot of time on 3-footers. I felt that if I could stroke the ball well on a long putt, the same stroke would work on a short putt.

Also, if I made any mistakes, they would show up a lot more on a long putt. For example, if my head or body moved or if I didn't hit it solidly, it would be much more obvious on long putts. On a short putt your head may move or swivel a bit, but you're not really sure because the stroke is so small. You only have a short time to feel it and really, you're just guessing.

If I was working on something in my stroke, I felt if I could do it on long putts it would automatically happen on the short ones. For example, if I could keep my head steady on long putts, it was going to be steady on short putts.

If my practice session was going well with long putting, I would take one ball and putt to one hole at a time, as if I was putting on the course. In other words, I'd take a long putt and then try to make the second putt. I took it quite seriously. The intent was there.

Think Your Way Around the Golf Course

THINKING MY WAY around the golf course was very important to me. I took it very seriously and it was a big part of the reason that I was able to win so many tournaments. It made me feel so good when Mickey Wright said that I managed a course better than anyone she ever played with.

There are three main things that were important to me in course management.

The first was to identify trouble and to hit away from it. I'd look for out-of-bounds, water hazards, fairway bunkers, and deep rough and so on. I'd get the lay of the land to see how the ball would bounce and if fairways were hard or soft. I'd look to see what was over the greens, which greens held the ball and which ones didn't, if there were difficult up-and-down situations to avoid, and if it was better to miss the green short or long. Then I'd hit away from it.

Next was to identify the area where I wanted to hit the ball so it would be in good position for the next shot. I'd ask myself, "Where do I want my ball to end up?" For example, there might be a section of a fairway that was wider or that gave me a better look at the green.

And finally, I played a shot that I could play. Let's say that the perfect second shot on a par 5 was a hard hook with a 3-wood. I would still play a fade because I had confidence in my fade and there was a better chance that I would hit a good shot with it.

Hitting away from trouble, hitting the ball in good position, and playing my highest percentage shot were my three rules for thinking my way around the golf course.

Lies Tell the Truth

THE LIE MAKES all the difference. If your lie is good all options are open to you. If it isn't, your options are limited. The lie dictates what you can do on the course.

When you're in the fairway, hopefully you'll have a decent lie. But even then, your ball may find small variations which are important to consider. Your ball might be sitting in a little cupped area, on thin grass, on a firm fairway, or in an old divot that's grown over with higher grass. In those cases and others, all options are not open.

When the ball is sitting up on a nice cushion of grass, well, those lies you just pray for. If you get that lie, it's just like the ball being teed up. You can hit any type of shot you want.

But let's say the ball is sitting down on a firm fairway. It's going to be harder to finesse a ball out of that lie. A high shot off that lie would be tough, but it wouldn't be that difficult off a good lie on a soft fairway. But there again, you need to say, "A high shot off this lie is not a good shot to try."

That's why you have to know your capabilities and your swing. You must know what your most reliable shot is from different lies. Even the best player in the world would have a hard time with a high shot off hardpan.

The lie dictates what shot you play. If the shot calls for a nice, high, finesse shot, and you've got hardpan, you're out of luck. Your shot selection has to change. You must say to yourself, "I can't hit that shot from here. What shot will give me a better chance to get on the green."

Your lie in the rough is also a big factor. The depth of your ball in the grass, the amount of grass behind your ball and the direction that the grass is growing are only a few considerations. How the ball sits dictates a lot of things that you can and can't do.

One tip for the rough is to set the club down behind the ball. If the clubhead sinks lower than the ball, you know you have a cushion underneath it. If the club and the ball are both down to ground level, you have to take a different swing. Remember, you're setting your club down. You're not pressing it down.

The lie is also very important for chipping and pitching. There are so many variables involved. They say that there are so many different lies around the greens in Scotland and Ireland that every time you miss a green you have to invent a shot.

If you have a bad lie you don't have many options. When you have a half-bad lie, you're still limited. Practice and learn what shots you can play from different lies. You have to do what the lie tells you because lies tell the truth!

Sidehill Liars

THE BOOK CALLS a sidehill lie towards you a "Hook lie" and says that you're going to pull the ball. The book says the opposite for a sidehill lie away from you. It's called a "Slice lie" and says you'll push it. Did the book ever hit these shots?

When the lie was sidehill away from me, I rarely pushed the ball because knowing what the book said it will do, I did everything I could to prevent it. When I had a hook lie with the ball above my feet, I'd fight against a pull and usually hit it to the right for the same reason. When playing a shot, knowing your natural tendencies is more important than what the book says.

Ball position is very important on sidehill lies. That's why I took practice swings. Where the club hit the ground was where I played the ball in my stance.

When I had a sidehill lie towards me, the ball was closer to me so I'd choke up a little on the club. It's more of a baseball-type flat swing. When I had a sidehill lie away from me, I'd bend my knees a little more so I could get down to it, because the ball was farther away. You have to make adjustments, but your adjustments must feel comfortable and balanced.

On uphill lies, you'll need more club because it's harder to get to the ball and you'll hit it higher. On downhill lies, take a little more lofted club. I think that's probably the hardest shot, but once again, just try to be balanced. Take a few practice swings to feel your balance and to see where the club hits the ground.

Also, know that you're not likely to hit your career-best shot. Play a little safer. It's also important to accept the lie without getting upset. Do the best you can. Also, if you practice sidehill shots, they won't be as much of a panic situation.

Another factor is that you don't have to play these shots very often. Maybe you do up north, but usually fairways are pretty level. Still, whenever you encounter an adverse condition, the most important thing is balance, balance, balance.

You really have to practice if you try to work the ball off sidehill lies. For example, with a sidehill lie towards you, fading the ball by crossing the line is a very difficult because it's more of a flat swing. You have to do some serious practicing on sidehill lies to learn how to work the ball off of them.

Ball position and balance are so important. You might want to bend one leg more than the other, or lean a certain way, but the main thing is to maintain your balance and to find the correct ball position. The best way to do that is to take a few good practice swings.

The book might be right in predicting where you'll hit the ball, but sometimes it could be a sidehill liar.

Find out for yourself.

Serious Practice Swings

HARVEY CALLED IT "INTENT." He never wanted me to take a practice swing without intending to hit something. It could be a tee, a leaf, a blade of grass, or anything, but he wanted me to try to hit something because you're trying to hit something when you're on the course.

He felt that a practice swing was practicing for playing on the course, so you should make both situations as closely related as possible.

A practice swing can also be valuable on sidehill lies to find the correct ball position and around the greens to get a feel for the grass and your lie. Is the lie fluffy, thick or clean? Knowing the thickness of the grass gives you an idea of how hard to hit the ball, and what shot you're able to play. You see pros take practice swings around the green all the time.

To Harvey, just swinging without trying to hit something or feel something was a waste of time.

The Goal is to Win

WHEN YOU BOIL it down, if you play your cards right winning takes care of itself. But the goal is to win. The reason I went through the process was to win. I knew that if I went through the process correctly, it would increase my chances of winning. And winning was what it was all about.

At the beginning of my rookie year, if a person came up to me and said, "Someday you will have more official tour victories than anyone in the history of the game," I would have thought that person was crazy.

You never know!

Don't Hit a Shot that You Haven't Practiced

HARVEY SAID, "DON'T ever hit a shot that you haven't practiced." That was great advice. I couldn't imagine jumping up and hitting a shot that I didn't practice and wasn't sure about.

Not that I always chose the right shot, but at least I had practiced it. I wasn't just trying to hit a new shot without knowing where the ball would go.

There weren't many shots that I backed away from on the course, because I had confidence that I could hit them. That's why those clinics with Patty were so valuable. We practiced and hit almost every shot there is to hit.

Harvey's advice was great and I never went against it. Luckily I practiced just about all of them.

Oh My, What Were They Thinking?

WE'VE ALL SEEN it happen. A tour player is coming down the stretch with a fairly big lead and somehow they blow it. They take bad swings, use the wrong clubs, hit the wrong shots, miss putts, and make bad decisions.

We say to ourselves, "What are they thinking?"

Actually, the answer usually is, "They're not thinking." Or if they are thinking, the answer is, "They're not thinking clearly."

The trick is to realize that it's happening and to "Snap out of it!"

I'm Too Busy to Talk

———

AFTER I HIT a shot, unlike a lot of players, I didn't chit chat with my playing partners as we walked down the fairway. It's wasn't that I was anti-social. Actually the reason was that I was too busy to talk.

There were so many things on my mind. For starters I was in the heat of competition and when I was in a competitive frame of mind, I just wasn't in the mood to talk. But even if I wanted to visit, it would distract me from thinking about what I needed to do on the next shot. If I'd hit a bad shot, I couldn't think about what I did wrong so I didn't make that same mistake again during the round.

In terms of my ball, as I walked I looked at its position, which gave me an overall view of the next shot. I reminded myself about the hole in terms of places to avoid and safe places to hit. Next I thought about the club that I might hit and the type of ball flight if I had a good lie.

Thinking about those things as I walked down the fairway was important because when I arrived at the ball I was ready to do the final calculations. First was to look at the lie of the ball, because even in the fairway you could get a thin, cuppy, grassy, or other type of lie.

Next was getting the yardage. The wind, elevation, and the firmness or softness of the green had to be factored in as well. After considering that information, I would determine the club and shot that would give me my best chance for success.

Tiger Woods doesn't talk very much when he's playing, either. It's not that he doesn't want to be friendly with the other players as he walks down the fairway, it's his competitive instinct combined with thinking about his next shot that holds his focus.

Personally, I don't understand how tournament players chat as they walk down the fairway. Maybe that's great for them, but I wonder if they're as prepared as they could be for the next shot when they get to the ball. Or, if the pace of play would be a little quicker if they were thinking and calculating as they walked.

After I hit my drive and walked down the fairway, I wanted to pretty much know where my ball was, the angle I'd be hitting into the green, the position of the pin, the wind direction and the club I would likely be hitting.

Anyhow, players said I didn't talk on the golf course and that's why. I didn't talk because I was too busy.

Never Blame Anyone or Anything

I ALWAYS FELT that it was totally my fault when I hit a bad shot. I chose that way to think because if I took responsibility for it, I could do something about it. I could improve when I was in the same situation the next time.

If I blamed something or somebody, I wouldn't see any reason to improve. After all, it wasn't my fault. If I accepted the responsibility, it made me want to fix it.

I'm the one who hit the bad shot. It's not the equipment. It's not the ball. If I had a bad lie, it's my fault because I selected the wrong shot, the wrong club, the wrong technique, or the wrong something for that lie.

I always enjoyed saying to myself, "I made a mistake, but I won't make it again."

If I was honest with myself, I could say, "What in the world was I thinking about when I hit that shot? Did I try to cut off more than I was capable of cutting? Was it the wrong club? Why didn't I take this or that into consideration? Did I try something that I couldn't do?" I'd ask those questions about every bad shot after each round and analyze my mistakes. When I thought that way it freed me up.

Playing well was due to course management and knowing my game. I couldn't do that if I continually said, "It wasn't my fault." How could I learn and improve that way? How could I play a golf course well if I continually thought that it was something else and not me?

I tried to learn as much as I could about my swing, tendencies, strengths, weaknesses, and course management. If I hit a bad shot, I'd ask, "Where did I go wrong? What caused me to hit that shot?"

For me, it all boiled down to taking the blame and evaluating my bad shots after the round.

The Fewest Mistakes (Usually) Wins

WHEN I FIRST went on tour, I got to play with the best players. Honestly, I didn't think that they would hit bad shots. They were great. They were famous. "What? Mickey Wright hit a bad shot? Never!"

At first it surprised me when I saw one of them hit a shot way off line, but it made me realize several things. The first was that everyone hits bad shots. The second was that although they hit a bad shot, they hit very few of them. And finally, it's the golfer who hits the fewest bad shots who is either in contention or wins come Sunday.

Everyone makes mistakes. Nobody is going to hit the ball perfectly all the time. Today you see some rounds of 61, 62, or 63 and in those rounds the players didn't make very many mistakes, if any. They might have made one or two but it probably didn't cost them anything.

But a tournament is three or four rounds. It's the total number of mistakes that matter. Mistakes add up.

You can't win a tournament in the first or second round, but you can certainly lose it. It's not just mistakes in the last round, although those are the mistakes that show up the most. It's the accumulation of mistakes from the whole tournament. No one plays four rounds without making mistakes.

There are always things that you can look back at and say, "Gosh, if I only played that shot in another way it could have been a different ballgame." Sometimes you only lose by one or two strokes so that mistake is magnified.

I tried to avoid mistakes by knowing where the trouble was, knowing where I could bail out, and playing my game. I did everything I could to avoid making mistakes because I knew that the golfer who made the fewest mistakes over the course of the tournament more often than not ended up the winner.

Paralysis By Analysis

THERE WAS A time early in my career when I was working on some things in my swing and I was hitting the ball really well on the driving range. But when I got to the first tee, I couldn't start my backswing. It was the most terrible feeling. I had so many things going on in my mind that I didn't know how to start the club back. It was a classic example of paralysis by analysis.

It was 1962. I won a tournament earlier in the year and I had been playing pretty well. The problem happened towards the end of the year in Salt Lake City. After I teed the ball I was just paralyzed.

I asked Mickey if paralysis by analysis could really happen. She said, "Yes, you can get paralyzed by thinking too much about your swing and not where you are trying to hit the ball." Mickey saying that meant so much to me. I thought that if Mickey said it, it must be true. That's exactly what was happening. That was when I became a player.

The cure was to think about the target while I swung the club. That totally freed me up. Then I could bring the club back. I could swing with confidence. It gave me a reference to hit the ball where I wanted it to go. It was amazing how much it helped.

I was so upset from what happened on the range that I stopped practicing for the rest of the year. It was scary to stand up on the tee box without practicing, but I just had to convince myself that it didn't work the other way, so I had nothing to lose.

I said to myself, "You've got to make yourself do this. Forget the swing. Forget everything. Pick out a target and hit it there. If you hit it in the boonies, go hit it from there." That's where Harvey's advice to "take dead aim" really came into play. All I thought about was aiming and hitting at the target.

I would warm up before playing but I surely didn't think about my swing. It was a great turnaround.

I feel confident now when I tell somebody, when they get to the first tee, swing thoughts have to go out the window. You can't be thinking swing. Oh, you might be thinking of one little thing to get it started like Nancy Lopez, who would think, "Low and slow," but that's it. If you think about your swing it's dead city. I know it was for me.

The following year, when I wanted to work on my swing I would do it on the driving range. But even on the range my last thought would always be the target. I might work on timing, the takeaway, or whatever, and hopefully practice would cure my mistakes. But my last thought was where I wanted to hit the ball.

I guarantee, when I got to the course there was no way that I would think about what I was working on during practice. I learned my lesson and I learned it big time!

Think of the target.

Check Your Alignment First

THERE WERE TIMES when I was hitting the ball solidly but it wasn't going at the target, both on the practice tee and on the course. When that happened early in my career, my first instinct was to try to figure out what was wrong with my swing and to start experimenting.

Later in my career, if I was hitting the ball solidly but off line, the first place that I looked was my alignment. Fortunately, more times than not, I was aiming incorrectly and was actually hitting the ball where I was aiming.

Think about it. You're on the driving range hitting the ball solidly, but it's going to the right of your intended target. As a result, you change your swing and you start hitting the ball at that target. What have you actually done if you were aiming to the right?

What you've done is change a correct swing and make it incorrect. The correct swing that was hitting the ball solidly where you were aiming was changed to an over the top swing to hit the ball where you haven't aimed! Not only have you made a correct swing incorrect, but you are also reducing the chances that this incorrect swing will work on the course.

The bottom line is that if you're hitting the ball solidly but not at your target, the first thing to check is your alignment.

Swing as if You are being Paid by the Hour

ONE OF HARVEY'S sayings was, "Swing the club as if you are being paid by the hour and not by the job." What he meant was to bring the club back slowly. Naturally you want to have good clubhead speed at impact, but if your takeaway is too fast it throws off your timing.

When the takeaway is too quick everything gets out of sync. Nothing moves together. Everything is trying to catch up. You have to build up speed in the swing. It's hard to do that if you start out fast. I've never seen anyone start the club back too slowly.

There are so many things that bad timing can cause. In general, the hands, arms, and body aren't swung with coordination. Not only does that make it difficult for the swing to be moving its fastest at impact, it also makes it more difficult for the club-head to be facing the target while it's moving down that line.

Harvey had a lot of sayings that made so much sense. "Swing as if you are being paid by the hour and not by the job" was one of my favorites.

Developing Junior Golfers

THERE ARE JUNIOR programs that can help young players. There are junior clubs to fit them and courses that encourage juniors to play. If a child really wants it, they can find a way. You can always drag your clubs with you wherever you go and find a place to play. Whatever their station in life, no matter the economics, a junior with the help of their parents can find a place to play and learn the game if they want to badly enough.

Also, what's really nice is that people see what they are trying to do and they'll want to help. Golfers enjoy helping golfers. I see it happen all the time.

I've also seen situations where a family might not be wealthy or might have other kids, but want to sell the ranch to finance their child in golf. I've told the parent or parents that when they sacrifice everything for one child, it puts a lot of pressure on them. You might feel that you are doing this child a great favor but it's not fair to the child, or for that matter, to your other children.

If the golfing child has a strong desire to make it, they'll find a way. It's probably a good idea to back off and not sell the house. Parents can get caught up to the point where they're putting unnecessary pressure on the child. It just isn't fair. If a child feels that they are doing it for the family, it can absolutely suffocate them.

Sometimes a parent will ask me, "How can I get my child to become a great golfer?" The first thing that I'll point out is that they will have to enjoy the game. If they're just doing it for the parents or for some other reason, while not enjoying the process, it isn't going to work. They have to be doing it for themselves.

Even if they're good athletes, they're going to resent it because it's not something that they want to do. They might not be aware of it, but they might feel that they are doing it because their parents want them to do it. I've seen this with children and I've seen it on the LPGA Tour.

The first step is that the child has to enjoy golf and also to enjoy the process that's needed to improve.

In the Beginning

THE FIRST TIME I played golf was by accident. I was 15 years old and I went to the tennis courts to meet my friends to play tennis. When I got there they wanted to play golf, so I followed along.

My first impression of golf was that I couldn't believe how bad I was. I was pretty good at sports and here was one where the ball was just sitting there and I could barely hit it. I guess my competitive instinct came out because I couldn't wait to go back and try again.

I played as much as I could for about a year before my parents decided that playing golf wasn't a fluke. As a result of them realizing that I was serious about the game, they joined a club so that I could play every day. It was a 9-hole course, Jal Country Club in Jal, New Mexico.

I was lucky to be able to play every day because juniors weren't always welcome on a golf course in those days. Juniors could usually hit balls on a practice range but it was hard for them to find a course to play. In most places a junior could take instruction, but unless you played, you really didn't know if your swing worked. Thanks to my parents and a junior friendly course, I had it all.

If I hadn't had Jal Country Club, I don't know what would have happened to me. My family wasn't golf oriented or wealthy enough to belong to a ritzy county club. When I think back I realize how fortunate I was.

I was also lucky that I grew up in a temperate climate where I could play golf year 'round. It got hot in the summer but it wasn't cold in the winter, and I played golf almost every day. That setup was something that I needed to develop my game.

Scoring Well When You're Playing Poorly

WHEN I WAS playing badly and nothing was working, I'd hit a shot that I knew that I could hit. I'd do whatever I had to do to hit the ball where I wanted it to go. In my case, I hit a block shot when all else was failing.

My block was a weak, push fade. The ball started to the right and then went farther right. It looked ugly and it felt ugly, but if I aimed far enough left I knew where it was going.

I think of Greg Norman when he lost the 1996 Masters. He had a huge lead with nine holes to go. It broke my heart. It was like he was in a fog. That's when you have to fall back to something that you know you can do.

If you know that you can slice the ball, slice it! If you can hit a hook, hook it! Hit a 5 iron off the tee. Anything! Work on technique later. Hit two clubs more than the yardage calls for. Play punch shots. Do anything to break the pattern. You might as well try, because you can't do any worse. If you hit it lousy, well, you were hitting it lousy before. You need something to break that syndrome.

You have to know your game and what you're capable of doing. Forget about technique. Forget about the swing. Forget about whether you're doing this or that. Just say, "Oh well, I have to hit it now, so I might as well do what I know I can do."

Do what you need to do to get the ball down the fairway. Do what you need to do to hit it on the green. That's all it amounts to. Ideally, you'd like to hit the ball better, but there's always another day. Never lose sight of the light at the end of the tunnel. There's always later to work it out. The world isn't coming to an end. You'll survive. You'll get through it. You just have to talk to yourself and play mind games. I did.

The trick is to say, "I know I can play *this* shot." Who cares how you do it? After the round nobody wants to talk about how you did it. They just want to know your score.

Try to keep it in the ballpark, somehow and somewhere. You might be exhausted when you get in. You might be flat worn out. But it's wonderful because even though you're not happy about the round, you'll know that you gave it everything you had. You didn't leave anything out there. You feel good because you know that you played smart.

Then the next day, maybe that same mindset of shot selection is still there, but with a better swing. You don't know why, but everything seems to go right. It can turn around in one day. One day you're hitting it lousy and the next day you're hitting it great, but now you're also thinking great. You can't miss anything, and even if you do it goes in the hole anyway.

But it's a discipline. It's something you have to work on. When you're playing lousy, hit a shot that you know you can control. Even if it's ugly, to score you have to hit the ball from point A to point B.

There's no room on the scorecard for pictures.

Beautiful Mistakes

IS THERE SUCH a thing as a "beautiful mistake?" I think there is. In fact, I think that all mistakes are beautiful because it gives you the opportunity to figure out why they happened and to avoid making them in the future. That's beautiful. Isn't it?

Of course there's a lot that goes into it. You have to realize that you made a mistake. You have to relive the mistake. You have to analyze it to see where things went wrong. And finally, you have to come up with the correct solution.

A mistake is not easy to correct but it is easier if you look at a mistake as being beautiful!

Mirror, Mirror on the Wall

THERE WAS A time later in my career when I didn't hit many balls on the range because I didn't feel that I needed to. I certainly didn't hit as many as I did in my first few years on tour.

One thing that I did quite a bit of throughout my career, though, was look at my swing in a mirror. I would always take a club back with me to the hotel room. If I was working on a certain move or trying to get my hands in a certain place, I'd watch it in the mirror and see what it looked like. I liked to have a visual of where the club was, so I looked in the mirror all the time.

I'd look at my swing in slow motion to see where the club was. Harvey showed me photos of players who had the club where it should be, so when I looked at my swing in the mirror,

I knew. Those positions gave me a feel so I'd know what to work on when I was hitting balls.

Mostly what I was looking at was the clubface to make sure it wasn't closed or open. I'd look at where my hands and club face were and compare them to where they should be. It was just a reaffirmation of my swing. Also, by doing it enough times, I hoped it would automatically translate to the course.

Over the years I scraped a few hotel-room ceilings and once even got my club stuck in one. But that didn't stop me from practicing in front of the mirror.

One thing I never did was ask, "Mirror, mirror on the wall, who has the greatest swing of all?" I knew better than to do that, because I'm sure the mirror would have told me, "Don't ask silly questions Kathy. You know it's Mickey Wright!"

Would You Rather be Lucky or Good?

A LOT OF people say that they'd rather be lucky than good. Personally, I'm not sure why a person would feel that way. I'd much rather be good than lucky.

I want to be in control of my game and in control of my own destiny. I would never want to depend on luck or a lucky bounce.

When I played a round of golf, I wanted to know that my golf game was solid and that if I played smart, I'd shoot a low score. I can't imagine going to the first tee thinking, "I hope I get lucky today so I shoot a low score." That just doesn't make sense to me.

Working on my game to the point where I have confidence that I have a solid golf game is much more appealing to me than needing to get lucky.

Don't be silly, I'd rather be good than lucky!

That being said, I wouldn't mind if I was good *and* lucky.

The Ball Knows All

THE BALL KNOWS where the clubhead is facing at impact and in what direction it's moving. Whatever the clubhead does, the ball will do.

The starting direction of the ball is determined by the direction the clubhead is moving. The curve is determined by where the clubhead faces in relation to that direction.

The ball told me how well or how poorly I was swinging and, more than anything else, told me where to start looking when I had problems in my swing.

For example, I knew that if the ball hooked, the face was shut at impact. If it started to the left and hooked, it meant that I was also coming over the top. I also knew what to look for in my swing if the shot was too low or too high, pushed or pulled, hooked or sliced.

Seeing the ball flight and knowing what my swing did to produce that flight was the basis for improving.

Ball flight was very important to Harvey. I once asked him about the use of video cameras, which had become very popular. He said, "There are some good things about video, but if I can't see the flight of the ball, I can't help anybody. They could be topping it or duck-hooking it and I can't see the shot from the video. Since I can't see the flight, I wouldn't know what to tell them or what to do to correct them."

The ball knows if you swing inside-out or outside-in. It knows if the clubface is open or closed. It knows your swing speed and whether or not you make solid contact. The ball can't speak, but you know what it's thinking just by watching it.

The ball knows all.

Try to Make a Bogey

———•◆•———

WHEN I WAS in trouble on the course, I might have had high hopes of hitting a miracle shot and making a birdie, but to be honest, most of the time I was playing for a bogey. Maybe if I got lucky I'd make a scrambling par.

One thing was for sure: I didn't want to make anything more than a bogey. It's just so hard to recover from a double bogey. It's a psychological thing. But by focusing on bogey, I wasn't trying to make some miraculous recovery and get into deeper trouble. I was guarding against making a double bogey or worse.

The main reason why I wasn't in a gambling frame of mind was that I had to be honest with myself. I knew that I wasn't swinging very well, or I wouldn't be in trouble in the first place. I didn't want to compound my problems by trying to hit a shot that I had no business trying. I just wanted to take what the trouble shot gave me and no more.

As I tell people, if you're not hitting it that well, you're probably not going to be able to thread it through a little opening in the trees. It's just not a smart shot. Play a smart shot and rely on your chipping and putting.

If there was a big opening, I might get near the green. If I got lucky, maybe I could get it on the green or, in rare instances, close to the hole. But if there wasn't a big opening, I wanted to get to a point where I could pitch up and at least get a bogey. After hitting a crummy drive, a bogey isn't bad.

Sometimes I made a par because I put myself in the frame of mind that "if I can put it up there less than fifteen feet from the hole in three, I might make a putt."

The mindset was for a bogey to be acceptable. It's okay to make a bogey after a bad drive because a bogey is a whole lot better than a double bogey. I'd tell myself, "Your swing is a little off. Just get the ball back in play and don't compound things by trying to hit a miracle shot. Play for a bogey."

Golf's Most Important Fundamental

YOU CAN'T SAY "All great players do this or that" because it isn't true. They all have different ways of swinging because of body types, swing philosophies, and natural tendencies.

There is one exception. The one thing all great players have is a good clubface position at impact.

Impact is golf's most important fundamental.

If it's Breezy Swing Easy

IN GENERAL, THE harder you swing when you're hitting into the wind, the faster the ball goes and the more backspin it has. As a result, the higher it climbs. This is especially true with the shorter irons. It's a similar principle that makes an airplane take off. The more speed it has, the more lift it will have.

The old cliché "When it's breezy swing easy" is absolutely correct. The trick to hitting into the wind is to swing easier and to take more club. If I was hitting into a strong headwind, I'd hit an easy 6-iron instead of a full 8-iron.

With crosswinds, depending on the situation, I would curve the ball into the wind for control or ride the wind for more distance. If there was a right-to-left wind and I needed distance, I would hook it. With a left-to-right wind, fade it.

If I needed to hit a softer shot hitting into a green, I would curve the ball into the wind to slow it down and to keep it from curving too much. If the wind was going left to right and the pin was on the left, I'd put hook-spin on the ball to keep it straight. The strength of the wind would determine how much I hooked it. The opposite was true with a right-to-left wind. If the pin was on the right with a hook wind, I'd cut it into the wind to keep the ball straighter.

If the pin was on the right with a left-to-right wind however, I would usually play a fade and let the wind drift it over. But if the pin was on the left with a right-to-left wind, I would usually still play a fade because a hook would just come in too hot.

Harvey always said that it's difficult to hit a soft shot downwind, so if you're between clubs downwind, take the shorter club and hit it harder. That's an exception to the breezy swing easy rule.

An advantage I had, even though I didn't know it at the time, was that I was able to work the ball. I thought everybody played different shots depending on the direction of the wind, but I found out that some of the players were locked into one shot. Imagine being locked into a hook with a right-to-left wind and the pin on the right side of the green. Even if you hit a good shot, it's going to run away, far left of the hole.

Having different shots in my bag made it easier for me to play in the wind. That's probably why I was usually able to stay in contention when it got breezy.

Even if you have all the shots, a good mindset when you're playing in the wind is to know you're not going to shoot your career round, and it's not going to be an easy day. Keep your patience and try not to get too unhappy.

Drills

HARVEY DIDN'T LIKE drills because he was afraid that the drill would become the swing. I remember him working on my follow-through to help me swing down the line and to square the blade at impact.

At the time I must have been swinging too much inside-out. He said, "Aim to hit it over the pitcher's mound but finish over the shortstop." It worked, but he would only let me do it three or four times. He'd say "That's enough."

As you can see, that drill could have gotten me to swing 'over the top' if I did it too many times. Also, if you take the drill to the course you're not focusing on where you want to hit the ball. You don't want a drill to become a swing.

Then there are some drills that can actually hurt a person, like the one where you keep a towel under your right arm. Think about Jack. Would he have become the player that he became if he had kept that towel under his arm? No way. Even for me, that drill was restricting.

Harvey knew people exaggerate and go too far one way or the other. He was always afraid of that and that's why he didn't do a lot of drills.

He didn't want the drill to become the swing.

Make Yourself a Better Putter

WHEN I FIRST went on tour, it didn't take me long to realize that I was a bad putter. When you don't make many makeable putts and three-putt more often than you should, you know you have to do something or you'll be off the tour in short order.

In fact, I think it was those first putting experiences that never allowed me to think that I was a good putter. But I did become a better putter.

It was painful when I would struggle to get to the green and then when I got there, I'd throw it away. That was not acceptable, so I made myself a better putter. I did that by spending a lot of time on the practice putting green.

Eventually my putting fundamentals boiled down to reading the putt, aiming, thinking about hitting the ball at the target, and getting the ball to the hole.

Putting is such an important part of golf. It can save you or it can hurt you. There are times when you make a long par putt and it turns your round totally around. There are other times when you have that same long par putt and three-putt it for a double bogey. That can also turn your round around, but in the opposite direction.

One thing was for sure, I had to make myself a better putter and I did.

Miss to the Fat Side of the Green

SOME PEOPLE SAY that they're shooting for the fat part of the green. For me, that wasn't true. I was always going for the pin. But if I made a mistake, I made my mistake to the fat part of the green.

If the pin was on the right side of the green, I'd aim a little to the left of the pin and hit a fade back to the hole. The worst miss was to overcook it and miss it to the right, short-siding myself. To guard against that, I tried to make sure that if I missed the shot I would miss it to the left. In other words, I'd miss it to fat side of the green.

To keep the ball from going right, I made sure that if anything, the path of the club coming through the ball was slightly to the left, crossing the line. That insured that if I didn't hit the shot I wanted, I'd pull the ball slightly to the left at the fat part of the green.

Since a fade was my best shot, if the pin was on the left I'd usually aim straight at the flag and try to hit a straight shot. Once again, if I missed it my miss would lie at the fat part of the green. In other words, the shot would either go straight or fade. If it faded, I'd be pin high, to the right of the hole.

I always tried to hit my misses to the fat part of the green or to a place where I had a better chance to get it up and down. I identified tricky or dangerous areas in practice rounds and tried not to miss my shots in those places.

Of course, there were many times when I'd hit a bad shot and this strategy went out the window. Fortunately it worked more often than not.

Look Up Early
and See a Bad Shot

IT HAPPENED TO me just recently. I had a pitch shot around the green. I looked up and hit it fat. I was mortified. I hate when I do that. I think I was out of the shot before I took the club back. But there's one thing for sure. That wasn't going to happen again that day!

When it happens to me, it's usually on short shots. It's a short swing and I come up. I want to see the ball get on the green and get close to the hole. Maybe I try to help the ball up, to get it where I want it to go, instead of staying with it and letting the club do the work. Consequently, my head goes up, my body goes up and the club goes up. I feel so stupid when it happens but I just have to get over it and hit it again.

If there isn't a saying, "Curiosity killed the shot," there should be.

Another cause of looking up is fear. You're afraid you're going to hit a bad shot and you want to help it. You're not confident that you're going to hit the shot solidly or that it will go the right distance or direction.

For me, the best thing to do is to take a few good practice swings. I go through my whole routine. I make sure I come through the shot. I feel my arms and the club go past my body instead of coming up. When I step up to the ball, I feel all the things that I felt in my practice swing and try to copy it. So why didn't I do that the other day? Like I said, it didn't happen again!

It's pretty much the same for full shots. Insecurity and fear make us want to see the shot a little sooner than we should. If you see that coming, take a serious practice swing and try to copy it.

It doesn't matter if it's a short shot, a full swing, or anything in-between. If you look up early you're usually going to see a bad shot.

Warming Up

————•◦•————

ON TOURNAMENT DAYS I'd usually get to the course about an hour-and-a-half before the round. For the first half hour I'd go to the locker room and put on my shoes and so on. Then I'd go to the driving range.

When I warmed up, I started with short irons and then moved on to medium irons, long irons, fairway woods, and then the driver. Depending on the course, I'd practice certain shots that I'd probably need that day. It might be a drive with a 3-wood, a certain type shot on a par 3, and things like that. I'd also practice hooks and slices with different clubs.

One thing was very important when I warmed up. I would always, always, always aim at a target. I'd "Take dead aim" and think about the target while swinging. I wanted to do as many of the same things warming up that I would be doing on the course.

Then I went to the putting green. I practiced putting for fifteen or twenty minutes. You had to be a little careful on the practice putting green because very often it was a different speed than the greens on the course.

Since there were no chipping areas or practice bunkers, after putting it was off to the first tee.

Traits of the Greats

———•———

THERE WERE THREE things that I saw in all of the great players.
1. They tried their hardest on every shot.
2. They knew how to hit every shot.
3. They never gave up.

Checkpoints when My Game was Off

———•———

WHEN MY GAME was off, I had a checklist of things to go through to help me find what was wrong. I knew that if there was one incorrect fundamental, it could cause several other problems. Harvey put things in the order of importance as they related to my swing.

First I checked the clubface. I made sure it was square in my hands and facing the target at address. That set up everything.

Alignment was next. I'd go through my pre-shot routine.

If my pre-shot routine was good, I looked at my timing. Sometimes I'd get a little quick. If my timing was okay, next was my takeaway. Was it low, slow, and straight back?

I'd go through those checkpoints and nine times out of ten I'd find the mistake.

Thanks Harvey!

Be Honest With Yourself

———•◦•———

IN ORDER TO IMPROVE, I felt that it was very important for me to be honest with myself. By being honest and not making excuses, I took a closer look at my game and identified the areas where I had weaknesses. Whenever I made a mistake I would attempt to figure out "Why?" and try not to make that mistake again.

You have to keep putting yourself on the line so you see your strengths and weaknesses. Then you have to be honest with yourself.

It was easier for me to judge myself in tournaments because mistakes smacked me in the face. Competition brings out the real you.

An important part of the process is to be able to accept yourself no matter what. Improving is so much easier when you are honest with yourself. There are no excuses and no feeling sorry for yourself. It is perfectly all right to make mistakes. Even the best golfers do.

You can't say, "I got a bad kick and that's why I'm behind a tree." You have to figure out why you missed the fairway in the first place and then say to yourself, "It doesn't matter why I'm behind this tree, what shot do I need to get back into play?"

I always tried to be honest about how I performed because I wanted to deal with my game objectively. After every round, I looked back at it with the mindset that "I could do better." I'd go through the round thinking about all the mistakes that I made and try to figure out how to avoid them in the future. Was it my swing? My club selection? My shot selection? And I learned to accept that my mistakes were nobody's fault but mine.

I had to be honest with myself if I wanted to improve.

On a broad scale, sometimes my mistakes were obvious. I was a terrible trap player and I knew it. I had to get better and Patty Berg was kind enough to show me what I was doing wrong and how to do it right.

Other times my weaknesses were less obvious to me until I observed the other players. I was fortunate to be able to play with the best players on the LPGA Tour early in my career. I'd watch them very carefully in terms of the shots they'd play and how successful they were. If they had a shot that was consistently better than mine, I'd say to myself, "If they can do it, why can't I?"

With the exception of some of the shots that Mickey Wright hit, like a high draw with a 2-iron that looked like it was shot out of a cannon, I felt that with learning and practice I could learn to hit all the shots the other players hit.

The first step, however, was to have my eyes wide open and to be honest with myself.

Putting Thoughts

MY MAIN THOUGHTS while putting were to hit the ball down the line and to get the ball to the hole.

What a great thought it was to get the ball to the hole. I didn't have to be concerned with how much to take the club back or how much to go through. All I was concerned about was getting the ball to the hole. It was such a relaxing thought.

I see people practice short putts bringing their putter back just so far. Then they get on the course and they're faced with a sixty-footer. They have to take a longer stroke and they wonder, "How much farther do I take it back?" I tried that method of putting and it didn't work for me.

Getting the ball to the hole is a thought I learned from Betsy Rawls. She was a marvelous putter. I saw so many of her putts fall in from the side doors with the ball just barely reaching the hole.

Betsy said that when she stood over the ball, she would visualize the ball on a line going towards the hole. It actually made her keep her head down so she wasn't apt to look up. She didn't see the ball going on that line, she just visualized it.

I looked at the hole and I looked back at the ball and said to myself, "Okay, I want to hit it down that line and get the ball to the hole." Then things happened by themselves.

If you can read the green correctly, aim at your target, hit it where you are looking, and hit it at the right speed, you're going to make a lot of putts.

True Confidence

EARLY IN MY career I didn't have much confidence, and rightfully so. After all, true confidence comes from success and I hadn't had any.

Some people are able to produce confidence by using mind games. Somehow they tell themselves that they're good at something and they feel confident. To me that's false confidence. They might feel secure when they are standing over the ball, but it doesn't help them to hit better shots. Then they hit one bad shot and their confidence is gone. At least that's the way it would happen with me.

True confidence comes from success. If you hit a shot well time after time, or if you score well time after time, you'll develop true confidence. For that to happen, it boils down to knowing the fundamentals, practicing, always trying to improve, and being honest with yourself.

Walt Garrison, a retired football player from the Dallas Cowboys was asked, "Is it important to tell yourself 'Yes I can' to gain confidence?" I love Walt as well as his answer. He said, "Only if you don't b.s. yourself. If you don't really believe you can, you won't. But you could tell yourself 'yes I can' all day but if you don't have the talent and ability, it's not going to work."

True confidence comes from success and success comes from dedication.

Gamble or Play it Safe?

IF YOU'RE GOING to carry over water, cut a dogleg, try to hit a difficult iron shot close to the hole or charge a putt, you have to decide if it's worth the risk.

You have to decide that's what you want to do, because once you decide you have to commit to the shot. You have to believe you can be successful and understand that it might not work. You have to be willing to take that risk.

There are times when you don't have anything to lose because you're coming down the wire and everything is on the line. You've got to take that risk because if you pull off the shot, you have a chance to birdie the hole and win. If it doesn't come off, you weren't going to win anyway. It's now or never. That usually happens on the last few holes in the final round. That's a gamble that I would take every time.

Early in the round or early in a tournament, if a player has a lot of confidence in their game, they might gamble because even if they are unsuccessful, they have time to make up for it.

But keep in mind, tournaments cannot be won in the beginning, but many tournaments have been lost early on.

Personally, I didn't gamble a lot. I've hit shots from trouble that maybe I shouldn't have hit, but I never thought of that as a gamble. I hit the shot because I thought I could pull it off. Sometimes it was an eye-opener and I really shouldn't have tried that shot, and I learned not to try it again. I just never thought about that as gambling.

Gambling is just risk and reward. To be honest, I wasn't much of a gambler. I was a percentage player. I always was and I always will be.

Tell it to a Tree

THERE WERE TIMES when I was playing poorly, getting upset, and making bad decisions. When I recognized that was happening, I'd have to vent my frustration and give myself a pep talk to try to get things back on track.

What I did was walk into the woods and tell it to a tree. I'd say something like, "What in the heck are you doing? You could do better than this! Come on, let's get it going, and let's start right now!" That was the gist of it but my language was a little more colorful.

I had to bring myself back to one shot at a time. I'd focus on that and not think about anything else.

So far trees have never talked back to me, but I'm not taking any chances. For that reason I try to keep my drives out of the woods.

Admit it When You're Nervous

WHEN I FIRST went on the tour I was nervous about everything. I thought the world was watching me. In reality, the others players were so busy with their own games they were not only not watching me, they didn't even know I existed. But since you're so aware of yourself and your feelings, you think everyone notices. At some point you realize they're not watching and you get over it.

The first time I was in the lead of a tournament, I couldn't sleep that night. I asked myself, "What am I going to do now?" I was so excited about it. But that was solved quickly because I didn't stay in the lead very long. The next day took care of that.

On the course you play through these things and learn how to react when there's pressure. You say, "Oh, I'm not going to do that anymore. I still might be nervous but I don't have to fall back into the same mistakes."

I tried to go into the routine of denying to myself that I was nervous, but I couldn't. That's where players get into trouble. I remember some players saying "I'm just going out and having fun. I'm not even going to think about winning. Whatever happens, happens."

That doesn't work. Invariably, the players who said that folded. Not just once, but time and time again.

I always knew that if these players were leading a tournament, I had a good chance of making a run. They were so nervous, but said that they weren't going to let it bother them. When they missed a shot it seemed like they were singing to themselves, "La di da di da." Let me tell you, some of them sang whole concerts!

Of course the worse they played, the worse it got. I would be concerned when some of these players were two or three shots behind, because they could make a run for it. One player in particular would get aggressive when she was a few strokes behind and could really get it going. But when she was in the lead she was the lead singer in the band. La di da di da.

You have to admit it to yourself when you're nervous. It's okay to get nervous. Everyone gets nervous. Admit that you're nervous and learn to play when you feel that way. Then you can take a lot of pride in knowing that you played well under pressure.

That's where you build your confidence. You say, "Wow, I played well under pressure." It's a pat on the back. Acknowledge it when you're nervous and learn to play when you feel that way. I actually got to the point where I enjoyed the feeling of nervousness. It was thrilling!

If you're in contention and you hear the leader say that they're just going to go out and have fun in the final round, wear your nicest outfit on Sunday. You just might be up there at the awards ceremony.

Admitting it when you're nervous is the first step towards not allowing it to affect you.

Pat Yourself on the Back

IT'S IMPORTANT TO give yourself credit when you deserve it. That's one of the ways to develop confidence. If I hit a very good or great shot, especially if it was under pressure or in a difficult circumstance, it would thrill me no end. I'd think about it after the round and relive it time and time again.

Take pleasure in good shots, knowing that you did it. There might have been a hard shot for me but if I pulled it off, I was just tickled pink. I told myself, "I did it and I'm proud that I did."

You should take credit for hitting good shots and for playing well. That's where you build your confidence. You start thinking, "Hey I can do this. I'm not perfect. I'm not great. I make mistakes. But I can play." It's important to acknowledge that. "I hit this shot and this shot and I could do it again. I know why I'm here."

Don't get so happy that you don't keep trying to improve or that you get a big head. But absolutely, pat yourself on the back when you deserve it. It's important.

Playing Your Natural Mistakes

THERE WERE TIMES when I would play my mistake instead of fighting it all day. If my normal shot was a fade and I was hooking everything, sometimes I just went with the hook.

This happened once with my putting at Pleasant Valley C.C. in Sutton, Massachusetts. For some reason I was pulling all my putts to the left. I tried to fix it but I couldn't. It really showed itself on long putts. Every putt was left, left, left.

Somehow I was scoring fairly well and on the final hole I had a 40-foot putt for birdie. If I made the putt I'd win the tournament.

It was a straight putt, but since I was pulling them left, instead of aiming straight at the hole I aimed about two feet to the right. As it turned out it was a perfect pull. It went into the middle of the hole for a victory.

There are times when it's better to play your mistake than to fight it.

The Joy of Learning

IN GOLF, YOU can always learn something new. Harvey would say, "I learn something new every day." I really believe that he did. He enjoyed learning so much that he also said, "If I ever stop learning I want to quit."

If you think you know everything, what fun is that? There's nothing left out there for you. I always enjoyed learning something new.

Harvey spoke at many PGA functions. In addition to speaking, he would listen and take questions. Sometimes there would be a question and he'd say, "I don't know. I'll have to figure that out." He would figure it out and get back to that person. I thought that was great.

It's so much fun to learn.

How to Keep it Going When You're Playing Well

SOMETIMES A GOLFER will have a good front nine and when they hit the back they get defensive. A golfer shooting 32-42 is not unusual. As it turns out they can hardly wait for the round to end because they're making one mistake after another.

It happened to me several times. I got over playing defensively after a good start by asking myself the following questions.

Why would I want to change my strategy when what I'm doing is working?

The round isn't over, what am I trying to protect?

Nine is just a number, why should I change my strategy after that number?

That led me to the mindset, "I'm playing well. It's not over. Keep it going!"

How to Get Out of a Slump

WHEN I GOT into a slump, usually a fundamental had gotten out of whack. What I did was to go back to the basics.

I didn't want to mess around with my swing when I got in a slump. When I went there early in my career, I changed this and that and hit the ball worse. That was followed by second guessing myself and my confidence went out the window.

Then I realized that since I had it before, I could get it back again by doing those same things. The best way to do that was to go back to the basics and to do each part very carefully. The answer was not inventing a new swing.

It felt like taking baby steps, but what alternative did I have? I didn't want to go fishing for a cure because that messed me up even more.

Finally, if I couldn't figure it out myself, I'd acknowledge that and I'd go see Harvey.

Thank goodness for Harvey.

Are You Trying in the Right Way?

THERE ARE MANY golfers who try quite hard, but they're not trying in the right way. It's sad. They're giving it all they've got, but they're giving it in the wrong direction.

An obvious example is the player who is a very good ball striker, but is not a very good putter. You might see that person on the driving range hitting ball after ball, but they spend very little time on the practice putting green. But if you asked them, they'd say that they are going at it the right way.

It's so important to know what to work on to become a better player. That's where I was so lucky to have Harvey. He always pointed me in the right direction.

Don't Feel Sorry for Yourself

YOU CAN'T FEEL sorry for yourself on the golf course. You can't think poor me. You can't pout because the ball went here and it should have gone there. You can't say to yourself, "Why is this happening to me?"

Don't allow yourself to go there because it becomes a disease. It's going to hurt you in the present and in the future. Thinking that way feeds on itself.

When you start feeling sorry for yourself, you start giving up. You think, "No matter what I do the ball isn't going to go where I'm aiming." If you start thinking that way you might as well walk in because the worse you play the more you're going to feel sorry for yourself. It compounds itself.

If I saw that I was feeling sorry for myself, I'd have a little talk with myself and say, "Hey, snap out of this. You can do better than this and let's start right now!"

I Don't Like Roller Coasters

SOMETIMES TOUR PLAYERS get criticized by the media and fans for not showing enough emotion. I understand that from their point of view. It adds drama to see players elated and disappointed. It makes for good theater.

The problem for the player is that it's an advantage not to feel the extremes of emotions and not to wear their hearts on their sleeves. The reason is that if you get down, it's hard to bring yourself back up. If you're up, it's hard to bring yourself back down. In either case, you're more likely to make mistakes.

You don't want to get on that emotional roller coaster. It actually takes energy to keep yourself in check but it's worth it. You might think, "I did a great job over there. What a shot!" But you can't let that overtake you and let elation take over.

Or the other way around, you can't get down after a bad shot. You might try to figure out what you did wrong, but you just have to concentrate on the next one. You have to keep your mind on the present and not let past good or bad shots interfere with the shot at hand.

I remember going up and down. Up and down. Up and down. I learned to like smooth highways a lot more than roller coasters.

Winning Takes Care of Itself

EVERY TIME I played golf, my goal was to win. But winning took care of itself if I played well. Playing well meant being prepared and knowing that I could execute the shots.

It didn't help me to walk down the fairway saying to myself, "I'm going to win. I'm going to win." In fact, if I did that it would put pressure on me and I would play worse.

So here's the formula: You can win if you play well. To play well you have to execute shots. To execute shots you have to work at them. To work at them you have to learn how to hit them and to practice. If you learn and practice you'll win.

I'll see you at the practice tee!

It's Fun to be Nervous

IF I HAD a chance to win a tournament, I'd get nervous and excited about what was going on and what might happen. If it was the last day and it was going down to the wire, there was a lot riding on each shot and there was no tomorrow. It was all up to me if I was going to win or lose. I enjoyed that so much.

It was different early in my career. I didn't know how to handle that feeling. Later on when I got nervous in that situation, it was a fun nervous. It wasn't like "Ha, ha, ha," fun. It was fun in the sense that I had the opportunity to achieve my goal if I could keep it going. I knew that I'd feel great satisfaction if I pulled it off. That made it fun.

Everyone feels nervous energy when they're in contention and each individual handles it differently. Some handle it better than others. I always thought it was exciting and looked forward to being in that situation.

Sometimes I pulled off the victory and sometimes I didn't but it was fun and exhilarating to feel that kind of nervousness.

Stay in the Hunt

THERE WERE TIMES when I came in first place, but I really didn't win. On those occasions I came in first because somebody else lost. Somebody had a bad day.

Let's say the leader or leaders start making bogies or worse, but since you were in contention, the victory fell into your lap. I've been on the receiving end of some of those. That's why it's important to always put yourself in position to be in the hunt on the last day.

One of the girls on the tour was finishing second a lot and she asked me if I knew how many times I had finished second. I didn't know so I went back and counted. It was somewhere in the eighties. That's just a statistic and it doesn't really matter. But it piqued my interest so I checked it out.

The point that I'm making is that I was in contention a lot of the time. Finishing second was only an indication that I was close. I don't know how many times I finished in the top ten.

Then I thought about why I was able to be in contention so many times. The main reason was that I could hit a lot of shots. I didn't have to wait for a golf course or certain conditions to suit my game. My game could suit the golf course and the conditions. Some I played better, but I felt confident on any course we teed it up on.

Getting back to the main point, it's so important to keep trying because you don't know what's going to happen. After hitting a few bad shots you might think you're out of contention, but you really never know.

My very first tournament win came that way. I wasn't that far away from the lead going into the last day. I had a nice round, but nothing special. I sat in the clubhouse and Sandra Haynie bogeyed the last hole and somehow it fell in my lap.

To this day Sandra says, "I three-putted the last hole to let Whitworth win her first tournament."

How many times has a golfer stopped trying their hardest only to lose by one or two strokes? Has it ever happened to you?

Keep grinding. You never know.

Stay in the hunt!

Practice Rounds

IN PRACTICE ROUNDS, I didn't think very much about how I was going to score that day. I was looking at any number of things that would be important for me to know for the tournament, thinking that I'd save my good scores for when it counted!

Locating the trouble was first. I looked for the places to avoid like water, out-of-bounds, deep rough, fairway bunkers, and things of that nature. I wanted to know where they were, the distance to them, and where I could bail out.

I looked at the greens. I wanted to know which way they ran. Did they slope up, down, or sideways? What was their speed? Would they hold a shot? What was over the back?

Knowing the layout of the holes was also important. I looked at the terrain and how the holes played. I looked at the long holes, short holes, if there were any lay-up holes and how much could be cut off on a dogleg.

Every course had a few small idiosyncrasies that were hard to notice in practice rounds. Unfortunately, it took playing in the tournament and hitting there before they smacked you in the face. Then you noticed them big time.

In practice rounds I wanted to get the lay of the land and knowledge of the greens.

First and foremost, however, I wanted to locate the trouble.

Pressure Putting

THINKING ABOUT MAKING or missing putts put pressure on me. The way that I eliminated that pressure was to go through my fundamentals, knowing that if I did those things the ball would have its best chance to go in. I learned how to stop thinking about making or missing.

That was a turning point because when I thought about making or missing a putt, the pressure stiffened me up, made everything a lot more difficult to do and I made fewer putts as a result.

When I concentrated on lining up, hitting the ball at the target, and getting the ball to the hole, I made a lot more putts. I knew that if I did those things it gave me my best chance to make the putt and that mindset freed me up.

You wouldn't be putting if you weren't trying to make it, but you don't have to think about it. I just thought, "If I miss it, well oh well, I'll just have to hit it again. Now let's just concentrate."

So don't think about it. There's no reason to think about making or missing. It only puts added pressure on you.

Turn Anger Into Birdies

WHY DO GREAT players make a birdie after a bogey as often as they do? They make a birdie because they're upset that they made a mistake. They made a bogey that they shouldn't have made and they're going to make up for it.

The difference between a great player and a player of a lesser degree is that they turn their anger into determination instead of letting their anger turn into depression. They go to the next hole and say, "I'm going to beat it this time." They put their mind right back to what they are trying to do. They use their anger to concentrate more clearly.

My trick for turning anger into birdies was to realize that I made a mistake, then make up for it by trying harder. Anger got me to focus harder on the next hole as opposed to allowing it to upset my thinking, ruin my concentration and rushing the next shot.

Turn that mistake around into a positive. Turn anger into determination.

It's a mindset. You could make it work for you if you don't dwell on the fact that you made a mistake. Don't do that poor me thing. Say to yourself, "I made a mistake, and I'm not going to do that again. Now it's time to go the other way." It's a wonderful feeling because you're in control.

Don't let a bad hole dictate how you play the next hole in a negative way. The worst thing that you could do is to let anger distract you.

Manage your anger. Don't let anger manage you.

It's Easy to Quit

THERE WERE TIMES during certain rounds that I wanted to quit trying. It would have been very easy. But I kept trying and I'm glad I did.

It's very important to hang in there and keep trying. First of all, your round might turn around. But even more important, if you can keep trying when things are going badly, when things are going well your concentration will be at a higher level, and that's when you have an opportunity to really go low.

Don't quit. Hang in there. You'll be happy that you did.

Master Your Natural Shot

THE NATURAL SHOT for some golfers is a draw and for others it's a fade. They're just better at one than the other. My best shot was a fade and I never won until I started playing it.

It's important to be able to work the ball both ways at different heights when the situation calls for it. In fact, being able to do that was one of the main reasons why I could play fairly well on almost any course or in any weather condition. But most situations don't call for type shots.

Most situations allow for the opportunity to play a draw or a fade. That's why it's important to master one shot. Not that anyone will ever truly master a shot, but it's a big advantage to understand the fundamentals, to practice it, and to have confidence in the shot that comes easiest to you. It's good to fully understand one shot because you can always go back to the checkpoints.

It's great to have all the shots in the bag. But it's so important to have a go-to shot that you know you can depend on through thick and thin.

Master your natural shot.

The Goal of Practice

IDEALLY, THE MAIN purpose of practice is to take a correct swing time after time so it becomes grooved. You want to groove your swing so it will work automatically on the course.

There are so many things to think about when you're playing, and if possible, you don't want one of them to be your swing. The more your swing is grooved, the less you'll have to think about it.

When you're hitting the ball well on the range, keep hitting. The goal of practice is to groove your good swings.

Hold Your
Follow Through

————•◦•————

DURING A LESSON, Harvey asked me to hold my follow-through position. I held it and while I was standing there he came over and gave me a little shove. I couldn't keep my balance and sort of fell back a little. He said, "Let's try it again." The results were the same. He did it a couple more times, but I couldn't hold that position.

Then I thought, "You're not going to do this again." I was ready for it and I was solid as a rock.

Thinking about it, I realized why I was able to hold my finish. It wasn't only thinking about the follow through. Instinctively I knew it would be easier to hold if I started in good balance. If I had to be in balance at the end, it would make it easier if I was in balance at the beginning.

The same held true for the rest of the swing. I tried to maintain my balance throughout my swing in order to be in complete balance in my follow through.

Harvey saw that my whole swing was out of balance. Instead of saying I had to be in balance at address, on the backswing and so on, he just talked about the finish knowing that I'd have to be in balance everywhere to be in balance at the finish.

That was another example of Harvey's genius.

Show Business Got Me Out of Trouble

AFTER I SIGNED with Wilson Sporting Goods, I was asked to participate in their clinics. I spent six weeks with Patty Berg and we worked every day on what we'd do. Then we'd play tournaments on the weekends.

Six weeks of rehearsals. We'd work from eight to noon and then one to four or five in the afternoon. We'd rehearse what we'd do and say. It was like a show. In a year we might do forty or fifty clinics. They were mostly in the off-season, but if we had a week off we would do some.

We'd have to hit all the shots: hooks, slices, punch shots, sand shots, and things of that nature. Then we'd talk about it. But we'd have to execute the shots, so we had to learn how to hit them well. It was just part of the deal.

We'd hit high shots and low shots with different clubs, which was great because I'd learn what I could and couldn't do.

For example, I learned that it's not easy to hit a low short iron. You might have the right shot in mind, but you might not have the right club for the job. It's not easy hitting a 3-iron high. That is unless you're Mickey Wright.

I'm sure at some point when I was playing in a tournament I'd think, "I can play this shot. I've been practicing it and I was able to hit them in front of all those people. I should be able to hit it now!" It's not like I had more talent than anyone else, it's just that we practiced those shots a lot. And we executed them a lot. That was a great thing for the Wilson players.

Hitting all of those shots made me be a better player. It helped me be a better everything. It especially improved my biggest weakness. It made me a better trap player, and that was a big plus.

We practiced all these trouble shots, but I really didn't think that I got into that much trouble. Then one year I was voted, "Best Player From Trouble." There's no doubt that the clinics helped me, but I didn't realize it until Mickey made the comment that the exhibitions and the clinics really improved our games.

From those clinics I went from a very bad to a very good bunker player. I got to the point where I enjoyed bunkers from a good or bad lie. We demonstrated the buried lie, pancake, lip, downhill, and uphill. We had to hit all these shots in the clinics.

I know it made me a better player. When I went back on tour and was in trouble, if I had a backswing I pretty much knew that I was going to get it out and put it back in play.

I didn't realize how much I actually knew until I was paired with a really good player in a team event. We were on a short par four, dogleg right. She cut the corner too close and was in a little group of trees, but not really far from the green. It was hardpan and if she could hit it low she could pretty much roll it on the green, or at least near it.

There was a tree about a foot behind her ball and I said, "Take a 4- or a 5-iron, close it down, bring the club inside, and just give it a shove and get it rolling. You could probably get it on the green." She said, "I can't do that." I said, "Yes you can!" So we went through that again and she said, "I can't do that." I couldn't believe she said that she couldn't do that! I didn't say anything more about it and just said, "Well, do the best you can." I was just amazed. I thought that everyone could do that. But the reason that it was natural for me was because of the clinics.

Players can learn to hit these shots. Tiger Woods is always working on them. I saw a tape of a clinic that Tiger and his dad gave when he was a little kid. Tiger's dad said, "Tiger, hit a hook." Tiger looked up and said, "How much?" He was already into that when he was a kid.

It's something that you can learn. It was another one of those lucky situations I fell into by signing with Wilson. I became a better trap player, a better wedge player, better at working the ball, better at trouble shots, and better at everything. It was also the place where I learned to play my bread and butter fade. What's more, I became more comfortable speaking and being in front of people.

We tried to make the clinics fun. I'm not a good joke teller, so I didn't tell any jokes, but I tried to keep it light. I had a few quips to get the audience comfortable and to loosen up a bit myself. If a clinic gets too serious, it gets too slow. If everybody laughs a little bit it becomes a fun thing.

If I hit a lousy shot I'd make a silly comment like, "Sometimes you need that shot." If I hit a bad shot when we first started I would get embarrassed, but you get over that. You get used to missing a shot in front of people so you don't feel as bad.

It really helped me when I went back on tour if I was playing in front of a lot people. After all those clinics I hardly noticed the galleries.

It was just grand to watch Patty Berg in action. It was her production. We had a script which we had to write. We had to say it just so. We had to know our lines. The big message was to see your pro for lessons and to do it today. Also, it was a commercial for Wilson. We all had Wilson bags and Wilson clubs. It was just wonderful.

Patty asked me to help her with her clinic at the Women's U.S. Open. That was such a treat. It became fun for me and I felt that if I enjoyed it, the audience would enjoy it too.

Patty was very adamant, but it was great training. I learned so much from her. It was just another wonderful experience that just fell in my lap.

With all the big hooks and slices, high shots, low shots, and everything in-between, there is no doubt that show business got me out of a lot of trouble!

What a Difference
a Day Makes

ONE DAY EVERYTHING falls into place and you're playing great golf. The next day you can't do anything right. We all fight that. But why does that happen?

The main reason it happens is that our feel can change from day to day. One day you feel just great and you hit it great. The next day you might wake up and you don't feel as good. When you swing a club, even though the fundamentals of your swing haven't changed, it feels like they did and you can't break an egg.

To play consistent golf, you have to recognize that it's just a feel thing. Sometimes recognizing it is the hard part. You think your swing changed, but what actually changed is how your swing feels to you. What you felt yesterday you can't feel today.

When that happens, the next thing most golfers do is to start playing around with their swing. Then it's "Good night!" Believe me, I tried that and it didn't work.

For me, when my feel changed the only thing it changed was my timing. The way I felt changed the pace of my swing. For some reason I'd get quicker. I was usually a little antsy and anxious for some reason. Things weren't as calm.

That's when I had to recognize that my feel was different that day and I had to act accordingly. I would take extra care in my pre-shot routine and slow down my tempo. Maybe I'd take one more club. I'd start by slowing down my takeaway and remembering Harvey's words, "Swing by the hour, not by the job."

You have to trust that the swing is still there. You may not feel like it is, but it is. The trick is to recognize it and not to fight it. Do the best you can and don't get frustrated. Learn to live with it. Get through it, and maybe you'll feel better the next day.

Mental Practice

EVERY NIGHT WHEN I went back to the hotel room, I'd go through my round. The main thing I thought about were my bad shots. I'd try to figure out what went wrong.

While sitting on a chair or lying in bed, I'd think about those shots one by one. I wouldn't see the swing as much as I'd feel it. I could feel the address position, backswing, downswing, impact position, and follow-through.

I'd ask myself, "Was I coming down too fast? Did I take it back too quickly? What was my thought process? Was I too anxious? Was I focused on the wrong thing?" I'd bear down and many times I'd figure it out.

I also visualized my good shots. You need to feel them as well. I focused more on my bad ones, but you have to give yourself credit for the good ones too.

Visualization was a big thing for me. Another way I used visualization was in my mind's eye I could see myself on the driving range hitting balls. I'd see myself swinging with what I was working on, or what I needed to be working on. Then I'd go out to the range and try to do what I visualized in the room.

At times I could hit it pretty darn good in my mind!

I Didn't Like the Beach

WHEN I FIRST went on tour I was a terrible bunker player. It wasn't until I did the clinics with Patty that I knew what I was doing.

For me, the biggest thing in playing a sandshot was getting over the fear of following through. That's where practice came in. The position of the clubface at impact and how much sand you're going to take was important, but I had to get over the fear of taking a full swing. All of the good players had a full follow-through. Why didn't I?

Hitting and stopping wasn't working, so to improve I made myself take a full follow-through by intentionally exploding the ball over the green. Then gradually, I didn't hit it as hard.

The Purpose Is to Get the Ball in the Hole

MICKEY WRIGHT WAS a perfectionist. She wanted every shot to be dead, solid, perfect. If it wasn't, she would just get so ticked.

Early in her career, I was told, there were times when after a bad shot she would almost quit trying to win because she felt that she didn't deserve to win if she could hit a shot that badly.

Betsy Rawls had a conversation with her to help bring her back down to earth. The thrust of the conversation was Betsy saying "The purpose of the game is not to hit perfect golf shots. The purpose of the game is to get the ball in the hole."

It's okay to get a little upset at yourself if things aren't going exactly as you would like, but if you make a bad move playing chess, you keep trying your best to win. You don't knock over the whole board. Do you?

Fix Your Swing on the Course

I KNOW THAT I've said many times that while playing, I only thought about hitting the ball at the target. An exception to this rule, however, was if I was playing poorly and my swing fell into one its recurring mistakes.

If things got ugly, most of the time it was the result of one of my recurring mistakes and hopefully I had a cure for it. One mistake that I would make from time to time was swinging too quickly. For some reason my takeaway would get quick and that would throw off my timing. Bad timing would lead to other swing flaws and there was no way I could play my best golf that way.

If my swing got quick, I'd think about starting the club back slowly. In most cases, that would help my timing and correct the other mistakes that the poor timing produced. But I wouldn't think about it every shot for the rest of the round. I'd think about it on a few shots and that would set the tone.

Another bad shot that I would try to fix on the course was a solid shot that fell to the right of the target. That usually came from poor alignment. Nine times out of ten I was aiming to the right of the target and I just made sure that I lined up more carefully the next time.

You'd be surprised how often a golfer will fall into the same bad habits. It's a good idea to know what your bad habits are and to have a band-aid for them in case they crop up during a round.

What's the Worst that Could Happen?

THERE WAS A time when I was afraid to hit a bad shot and it reduced my chances of hitting a good one. I'd stand over a shot a say to myself, "I don't want to hit it here or I don't want to hit it there." It stiffened me up and I couldn't swing freely.

When I realized that this negative thinking didn't work and that I needed to change, I said to myself, "What's the worst that could happen? The shot will go way left or way right? Big deal, if it does, I'll just go there and hit it again!"

Realizing that it wasn't a life-and-death situation made me much more relaxed and helped take the tension out of my swing.

The Most Important Club

THIS IS WHERE Harvey and I disagreed. He always thought the putter was the most important club in the bag, but to me it was the driver. I felt it was the driver because I found that if I was driving the ball well, I was going to play well.

In order to play a hole with confidence, it starts with the drive. If you drive the ball in the fairway you can usually play the second shot the way that you've planned. If you have a good lie, which you usually will in the fairway, you'll be in control.

If you drive the ball in the rough, in the woods, or worse you're at the mercy of what the situation gives you. Hitting from the rough, working the ball around trees, hitting from a fairway bunker, or taking a penalty, to say the least, is not a good way to start a hole.

It's also a confidence thing. If I didn't drive it in the fairway, I felt that I was going to have a long day. If I drove it in the fairway, I felt more confident about my entire game.

I know that many people, including Harvey, think that a putter is the most important club in the bag. I agree that the putter is very important, but when I was driving the ball well, I usually played my best golf. That's why the driver was the most important club in the bag.

Longer Drives

THERE WERE TIMES when I wanted to hit the ball longer off the tee. And when I wanted to get that extra distance the main things I did were to grip the club a little tighter, stay in balance as long as I could, and come down a little faster through the hitting area.

I remember reading something that Jack Nicklaus wrote. He said that when he wanted to hit it harder, he would grip it a little tighter. I did that naturally, but it was nice to know that's also what Jack did. Jack wasn't exactly a short hitter!

I liked holding on tighter because I was coming through with more clubhead speed and I thought it helped. I also felt that a tighter grip made my hands stronger and allowed me to use more muscle.

That said, I didn't try to hit it very hard often, because I'd lose my timing. But when I did want to hit it hard, I gripped it tighter, swung harder, and tried to stay in balance.

The Will to Win

EVERYONE TRIES TO explain it one time or another. It can be called "Competitive desire," "Competitive instinct," or "The will to win." It's just something that's there. Even if you're not sure if you have it, you won't know until you find yourself in that situation.

I didn't know if I had the will to win. I knew that I had a great teacher and that I tried to get better. That's all I knew.

Early in my career I got into a sudden death playoff. I didn't win and I wasn't sure that I could win. But I kept trying. Losing didn't keep me from trying. Then it hit me, "Why would I be out here if I wasn't trying to win?"

All of my practice got my game to the point where I was in contention. That's when I realized I had the will to win.

Take a Lesson from Kathy

SINCE RETIRING FROM the tour, I've done a fair amount of teaching. I've taught in Japan and currently teach in the Dallas area at Trophy Club and at Grand Cypress in Orlando, Florida. I conduct three schools a year.

The following are some of the things that I've learned about teaching:

TERMINOLOGY

When you teach, you have to be careful with the terminology you use. Make sure your students understand your golf words and phrases. While giving a lesson, I kept using the term tight lie. After a while, the student asked, "What is a tight lie?" I just had to laugh and say, "Oh my gosh, I'm so sorry."

BE COMFORTABLE AT ADDRESS

When I first started teaching I asked students to feel like they were sitting on a barstool, to lean over and so on. It didn't work. They were too stiff and had too much tension.

Now I ask them to place their hands on the club with a square clubface, let their arms hang down, set the clubhead down to the ball, and take a comfortable stance.

When they do that their body naturally goes into a balanced and relaxed address position. From there it's easy for them to swing the club freely and with rhythm.

LET THE STUDENT FIGURE IT OUT

I like to point something out about a student's swing and give them the opportunity to fix it by themselves. I've found that if I let them try first, they just might come up with something. If they don't, they're usually more receptive to my advice.

GRIP AND CLUBFACE

One thing that I stress is the setup, and the setup starts with the grip and how it relates to the clubface. One of my favorite sayings is, "Hands on the club and a square clubface."

I ask them to watch the clubface to see that it doesn't open or close as they place their hands on the club. If it does open or close, they'll start over.

The more that I get people to place their hands on the club and check the clubface to see if it's square, the more they improve.

AIM AT TARGET

If you're aimed to the right or left of the target, it causes a lot of problems. Even if the swing is good, it causes problems because you're always trying to make adjustments to hit the ball at the target.

A lot of good things happen when you line up correctly and a lot of bad things happen when you don't. I get my students to carefully line up the clubface at the target and "take dead aim!"

THINK ABOUT THE TARGET DURING THE SWING

There's nothing that improves accuracy more than knowing where the target is and thinking about it during the swing.

I tell them, "Think forwards, not backwards."

THE TAKEAWAY

The takeaway can determine the downswing. If you bring the clubhead back on a straight line, it makes it easier to swing through on a straight line. If you don't bring it back on a straight line, it makes it more difficult to come through on a straight line.

The hands take the club back and it should be brought back low, slow, and straight back.

RESET YOUR GRIP

The more times you reset your grip and look at the clubface, the easier it becomes to do correctly and the sooner it will become automatic.

When my students are on the range I ask them to take their hands off the club after every shot and reset their grip. Sometimes they want to hold onto the club with both hands and reach for the next range ball. I tell them, "Let go of the club and reset your grip."

LET YOUR ARMS HANG

If you stood up right now and let your arms hang, they would hang naturally without any twisting or turning. That's the same way you want your arms to feel in your address position.

When you take your grip, place your hands on the club without twisting or turning your arms. Then as you address the ball, let your arms hang as you set the clubhead behind the ball. That will tell you how far to stand from the ball and how much to bend over.

A lot of good things happen when you just let your arms hang.

LEFT HAND GRIP

The left hand on the club is key, because it guides the clubhead through the hitting area. If it collapses, the right hand is worthless.

Without holding a club, just let your left arm hang. The position of your left hand should be in the same place when you hold the club. When you look at the back of your left hand while standing in your address position, you'll probably see three knuckles.

I always put my left hand on the club first.

BALL POSITION

To hit a good shot with bad ball position there has to be compensation in the swing. That's not good news.

The swing is an arc and an arc has a bottom. You want to place the ball at the bottom of the arc. For short irons, the bottom of the arc is generally in the middle of the stance.

Middle irons, long irons, hybrids, and fairway woods should each be a little closer to your front foot. As each club gets longer, the bottom of the arc is farther up. The ball position for the driver is in line with the inside of the heel of the front foot. The reason that ball is that far up with the driver is to catch the ball a little on the upswing.

I teach the routine that I use to position the ball in the stance:

Set the clubhead behind the ball and face the target, with your feet together. Place the ball in the middle of your feet. Depending on the club, step out different distances. For right-handed players, first step the left foot out and then the right.

Because you want the ball to be in the middle of your stance, for short irons the left foot and the right foot step out the same distance. Accordingly, the farther forward that you want the ball in your stance, the less you step out with the left foot and the more you step out with the right.

The total width of the stance should be less with the shorter clubs and a little wider with the longer clubs, but the total width should never be wider than the shoulders.

Everyone's swing is a little different. Finding the correct ball position for your swing is extremely important.

Where's the bottom of the arc for each of your clubs?

The Pressure of Being Number One

WHEN YOU BECOME the number one money leader, a lot of responsibility goes with it.

Every step of the way you know that you are a role model for somebody. I looked at the role models that I had: Mickey Wright, Betsy Rawls, Louise Suggs, and Patty Berg. I observed how they conducted themselves. It was always in a professional manner with high standards and integrity.

I didn't go around saying, "Oh gosh, I'm a role model," but I knew that my actions would affect somebody. So you accept that responsibility and you always try to do and say the right thing.

I was president of the LPGA four different times and when I wasn't the president, I served on the Players Board. I was on every committee except Treasury. They didn't let me handle the money because they didn't think I could balance the books.

Also, as the number-one money winner, you were expected to play in every event. The sponsors wanted the number-one player to play. It was an unwritten rule. You just did it. Mickey did it. Patty did it. Everyone did it. So when it was my turn, I did it. At times it was a burden, but it was the responsibility of being number one.

Every year it was my quest as the number-one player to maintain that status. That was the hardest part. Getting there was the fun part. I know that's a cliché, but it is true. But then the pressure is on you to stay there and it takes its toll. It eventually wears on you and sometimes you have to make a change.

When you're number one you have to be ready to accept the responsibility and some people don't want it. It actually scares them. When you win, whether you want it or not, certain things are expected of you. You're a leader and you have to accept the responsibility that goes along with it. Some people shy away from it. Believe it or not, for that reason, some people don't want to win.

There really is additional pressure when you're number one.

Clubhead Awareness

WHEN I LEARNED how to feel the clubhead and know where it was facing at each part of my swing, it helped my ball striking. After playing and practicing a lot, as well as looking at my swing in the mirror, I learned where the clubhead should be and how it should feel when it's there.

Of course the most important place was at impact, but it had to be in certain places at certain times to be square at the moment of truth.

Knowing where the clubhead faced was key when hitting shots. I always wanted my misses to be towards the fat side of the green. If the hole was on the right, for example, I played a fade. I tried to make sure that the clubface was a little bit open at impact, but if it wasn't, I wanted to err on the square or closed side, so the ball would be left of the pin. I could feel that and usually did it through clubhead awareness.

There were also times when I changed where the clubhead was facing on the downswing if it was headed for trouble. If there was a hazard or out-of-bounds, and I knew the clubhead was facing it as it approached the ball, I would turn it one way or the other to avoid disaster.

Being aware of the clubhead and knowing where it was facing helped me control the ball and to keep away from trouble.

When Trying Isn't Good Enough

As LONG AS you try, you have something to be proud of. All you can do is try your best, isn't it?

Some people try and maybe they're not as good as Sister Sue down the road, but at least they tried. As long as they try it's okay. What more could they do? They should feel good about themselves because they did all they could. Unfortunately it wasn't good enough, but they should still feel satisfied.

There were many tournaments when I didn't play my best, but since I knew that I tried my hardest, I felt good about it.

Trying is the key word.

If you try your best and don't make it, you might feel sad for a while, but it's okay because you gave it your best effort. How could you fault yourself? Be proud that you tried.

The Joy of Teaching

IT'S GREAT FUN to teach. A friend once told me that he gets goose bumps when he hits a good shot. When I help someone hit a good shot, sometimes I get them too.

When you see a golfer struggling and then you finally get them to hit a good shot, it's great to see them smile. That might be the only shot they hit well during the lesson, but I still get such a kick out of it.

I could see how Harvey got a lot of pleasure out of teaching. No matter the level of player, he enjoyed working with them. He enjoyed beginners as much as the touring pros. In fact, he might have enjoyed beginners more because they're so much more appreciative.

One time I had a lesson with Harvey and he told me what to work on while he gave another lesson. He went on to say, "These two ladies are here for a lesson because their husbands are getting ready to retire and they want to learn how to play." He went over there and after a while I could hear them giggling. He came back and I said, "How'd it go Harvey?" He said, "It was great. We got it airborne."

Now that I've had some teaching experience, I appreciate that statement a lot more than I did then. I know that for beginners getting the ball off the ground is such a revelation.

The Genius
of Harvey Penick

THE GENIUS OF Harvey was giving one simple tip that corrected your mistake and made about ten other important things happen automatically. Instead of getting caught up in mechanics, one tip would take care of all that. To me that's genius.

An example would be the tip he gave me for iron shots. I guess I was coming up a little at impact, so he said, "Clip the grass in front of the ball." That made me stay down, kept the clubhead accelerating through the ball, naturally released my hands, squared the clubface, kept the clubhead going at the target, made me stay behind the ball, and got me to hit with a descending blow. All that with one tip.

Harvey didn't tell me to get into any positions. He'd just say, "After you get yourself lined up, the last thought I want you to have is to clip that grass in front of the ball."

The genius of Harvey was to boil things down to very simple thoughts.

After I retired from playing on the LPGA Tour, I mentioned to Harvey that I wanted to do some teaching and he gave me some tips. The most interesting part was that he told me things to watch out for that he never mentioned when he was teaching me.

He never talked about the body turn, but when he gave me tips on teaching it was one of the first things that he said. I asked him, "Why are you talking about the turn now but not before?" He said, "I didn't need to because you did it automatically. You didn't need to know about it."

Harvey taught as simply as he possibly could. He didn't mention golf swing fundamentals if I did them automatically. Isn't that just wonderful?

Harvey was a genius!

Positively Harvey

HARVEY WAS A very positive person. He gave a positive spin to almost everything. At least he tried to without being dishonest.

For example, when I first went to him I was bringing the club way inside on my takeaway and then coming over the top. He said, "You could play that way, but it would take more work."

That's how Harvey made something bad seem a little good.

Having Rabbit Ears

SOME DAYS ARE different than others. It's weird, but on some days you hear everything. I don't know why, you just do. Someone could be whispering ten greens over and you hear them. It's just one of those days, but you have to recognize it and accept it. You might be thinking, "Why me?" But really, what can you do about it?

Galleries or marshals didn't necessarily bother me. They were doing the best they could. You know there's going to be noise and movement, especially if you're in the last few groups.

The worst was the photographers because they knew better. It was so irritating because they always wanted to get that one photo while you were taking the club back or through the hitting area. All you hear is this click. It's not the loudness, it's the suddenness and it's at the wrong time.

I don't know how Tiger Woods does it. There are cameramen running around trying to get behind him, galleries moving and making noise, and sometimes people are taking pictures. That takes some getting used to! But if he gets distracted, he steps away from the ball, gathers himself, and gets ready to hit as if it never happened. He's so good at that.

The trick is to know that there will be some distractions and not to let them bother you. If the distraction is so noticeable that you have to step away from the ball, be a Tiger!

Unsolicited Advice

THERE WERE TIMES when I was struggling when someone would want to give me advice about my swing. They had good intentions, but unless I asked for help, or if it was from someone that I respected, I preferred not to get involved with it.

Sometimes it's a challenge to find a polite way to tell a person that you aren't interested in what they want to tell you. One thing I've said was, "I appreciate your help, but I'm working on something."

Unless you really want to hear what they have to say, which I don't if I'm in competition, listening to their advice can do more harm than good. In fact, Harvey warned me about taking advice from others. He said, "Most golfers will teach you what *they're* working on even if it doesn't apply to you."

If I wasn't competing and I was hitting the ball poorly, maybe I would listen to what someone had to say just for the heck of it.

I might be curious about what they saw and their interpretation. But I was always very careful about whom I listened to.

There are many well-intentioned and sometimes not-so-well-informed golfers who love to teach. For that reason, if you aren't interested in hearing what they have to say, it's a good idea to have a polite way to say, "thanks, but no thanks."

Teaching by Asking Questions

THERE WERE TIMES when Harvey would ask me a question because he wanted me to figure it out on my own.

One time without knowing it, I had the face open at address. Instead of telling me it was open, he knew it would have more impact if I saw it myself. After hitting some shots, Harvey stopped me when I was in my address position. He walked over, took my club without changing its angle and stepped in my stance. I went to the other side and looked. He asked, "Do you think the face is open?" He left it up to me to decide. I thought it was and I said "Yes."

Of course he was leading me there, but by the same token, I could have said it looked square. It very well might have and if I said it looked square, he would have gone in a different direction.

There were several times when he would explain something and then ask, "What do you think about that?" He wanted to know if I understood what he said and whether I agreed or disagreed. If I understood and agreed we would move on. If I didn't, he would explain it in a different way.

It made me feel better about myself and more confident when Harvey asked me questions.

Two Points for Kathy the Teacher

I GAVE A lesson to a magazine writer once who had taken a lesson from Harvey. I knew he had taken that lesson, so I was thinking "Oh no, what am I going to tell him?"

He hit a few shots and I said, "If you would relax your arms and just place your hands on the club they wouldn't be all twisted, and the clubface would be square." He started to laugh and said, "I want to show you something." He took Harvey's book out of his golf bag and showed me a little message that Harvey wrote. The message was the same thing that I just told him. I just thought, "YES! I said the right thing."

Golfers Help Golfers

AT JAL COUNTRY Club in New Mexico, the nine-hole course where I learned to play, a group of guys including my dad financed me to go on the LPGA Tour. It might not have happened if they hadn't seen that I was really serious. They saw that I really wanted to play and to get better.

I was fairly good at that time, but the interesting thing was that people wanted to help. I've seen it happen so many times when a golfer will help another golfer. Usually it's someone who's trying really hard.

Maybe people want to help because the game is so difficult. If you work hard and show a willingness to improve, you'll get a boost here and there. You don't have to ask. People will just want to do it.

The Feel of Victory

I WOULD RELIVE a victory, but I wasn't able to feel it right after it happened. There's so much going on and it takes a little while to sink in. I'd have to wait until later when it was quieter.

We'd travel by car and as we drove I'd relive those moments. I'd think about what I was feeling while I was going through the last round. I'd think about the back nine, the last hole or two, a pressure shot, and what I was thinking and feeling during those situations.

You relive it, but then next week is another tournament. What you did that week doesn't matter. Whether you've won or lost, it's over. That's a done deal.

It's nice when family or friends are there to share a victory with you. When I won my first tournament my uncle was there and that was fun.

When I broke Sam Snead's record of 86 wins I was in Rochester, N.Y. That was my favorite place to play. I stayed with a wonderful family for about 15 years, Bill and Betsy Morse. I stayed with them that week as well.

I watched their kids grow up, get married and have kids of their own. We went to their lake house that Sunday night. I have pictures of it. It was so much fun.

It's was nice to be able to share victories with people, but it's a personal thing.

Golf is just one person. At least tournament golf is.

Most Improved Player (Twice?)

———◆·◆·◆———

TO BE VOTED the LPGA's "Most Improved Player," you must show more improvement than anyone else on the tour. I received that award in my second year and was proud to get it. In my fourth year on the tour, I got it again. Once again it was special.

Then I started to think about it. What does it really mean to get a Most Improved twice? I came to the conclusion, "Gosh, to win it twice, I must have had a long way to go!"

They were right. I did have a long way to go!

Men Champions

———◆·◆·◆———

LEE TREVINO

I played with Lee Trevino before he was *the* Lee Trevino. We did an exhibition in his hometown of El Paso, Texas. He was the pro at the course. Then soon afterward, he went on to win the U.S. Open.

When I played with him, I remember remarking to Carol Mann that he had a wonderful short game. He didn't hit the ball as long as some of the other men that we played with, but he had an exceptional touch with his putter and wedge.

Then he won the U.S. Open. I thought, "There you go. One day he's an unknown and the next day he's winning the U.S. Open." Of course it didn't happen like that, but it felt like it.

SEVE BALLESTEROS

In South Africa at the "Million Dollar Challenge," they had a women's division and I got paired with Seve Ballesteros. I thought, "This is pretty sweet!" It turned out that I was paired with him for three days.

It was fun to watch him play because he was still on top of his game. He was very gentle and kind, and very nice to play with.

Seve was amazing at getting out of trouble and he had a great short game. He was all over the place the first day and was an artist at getting it up and down. It reminded me of the year that he won the Masters when he was coming into the greens from everywhere, but it didn't matter because he got it up and down.

We played together for three of the four days and we were together again at the awards ceremony. We both won.

TIGER WOODS

I like just about everything about Tiger. He handles himself very well. Yes, he has a temper and at times I wish he would be a little more in control of it, but he gets angry because he's trying so hard. He's not angry at anyone or anything except himself.

It's so much fun to watch him because you never know when he's going to pull the shot off. You don't get that intensity with the other players. He's out there to win and he'll try anything it takes to do it.

He hits soft shots, hooks, slices, high balls, you name it. He's hitting more soft shots to the greens, which I just love. It's nice to have feel, and he also demonstrates it around the greens.

Even his mistakes are exciting. How about the 200-yard 9-iron he hit over the clubhouse at Firestone? I think his ball ended up somewhere between the swimming pool and the veranda. My first thought was, "Well, I guess he'll just have to settle for par!"

JACK NICKLAUS

Obviously Jack was a wonderful player. Some people talked a little about his wedges around the greens being weaker than other parts of his game, but he was such a good putter he made up for it. The rest of his game was just terrific.

I really wasn't able to watch Jack all that closely because we were playing at the same time. Our careers were almost parallel. But when I was able to watch him, I always got a kick out of it.

After winning a tournament, Jack once said that he wanted to be in control of the ball after it left the clubface. I understood what he was saying. He wanted to control where the ball was going, how it reacted when it hit the ground, and so forth. That would be nice, but I don't know if that's possible. He must have had a great round that day!

I remember the press and the fans really beating up on Jack when he first came out on Tour. They felt it was unacceptable that anybody beat the King, Arnold Palmer. Jack played through some tough galleries. Considering the hostility, it's what made Jack even better in my eyes. His attitude was, "Like it or not I'm here!" Jack wasn't backing off, but it was pretty ugly at times.

Jack just kept on playing and eventually won everybody over because of his ability.

ARNOLD PALMER

I was a big Arnie fan, but I didn't get to watch him play that much because, like Nicklaus, we played at the same time. When I was able to watch him, I liked seeing him get out of trouble. That was always exciting.

He was a great competitor and had charisma. He loved the gallery and the gallery loved him. The LPGA Tour and the PGA

Tour weren't that far apart in terms of the numbers of events and prize money until Arnold Palmer. He came along about the same time that golf was put on television. Arnie just made that thing explode.

Arnie's charisma solidified the PGA Tour and it just took off. Arnie was the catalyst and he was the main reason why they put men's golf on TV every week. There's no doubt about it. Arnold Palmer set the stage for what golf is today.

SAM SNEAD

Oh Lord, he was a great guy. I was fortunate to play with Sam a couple times, but I have to tell you, I had to set ground rules. Sam could be a little rough around the edges and tell some terribly crude stories.

But oh-my-gosh, what a great player. I mean to this day, if he was alive and 100 years old, he would probably make that same smooth swing. He was that good.

There was a mixed-team tournament with a senior division. He and I were still on the Wilson staff when his manager, Joe Phillips, called me and asked, "Would you like to play with Sam?" I said, "Well, I'll tell you what, Joe. I'll play with him, but he's done some ugly things. Mickey Wright once came into the clubhouse in tears. If he gets out of line, I'm walking off the course." Joe told Sam what I said and he was just great.

When I broke his record he called me and was very sweet about it.

GENE SARAZEN

I got to know Gene really well towards the end. He told me one time, "All my friends have passed away and I'm lonely." I felt so badly for him but the "World Championship" tournament at "The Legends," gave him some quality time. Gene was the host.

They had an opening ceremony the year the course was built. They had Gene, Sam and me out in the middle of all these trees.

We were "The Legends." It was one of those first shovels of dirt deals. Anyway, they said, "This is where the tee will be and we'd like for each of you to hit a few shots. We're taking pictures."

I hit a few shots. Sam hit a couple of shots. When it was Gene's turn he said, "I'm only going to hit this one time, so get it this time, or don't get it at all." Everyone laughed and he hit a nice shot down the middle.

Gene was fun to watch and it was always interesting to listen to because he had great takes on a lot of things.

Early Retirement?

I ALMOST QUIT the tour after the 1973 season because my nerves were giving out. I was exhausted. I finished the year as the leading money winner by winning the last couple of tournaments, but I was out of gas.

I had gone for #1 for about twelve years. Once I got there, I tried to maintain that level. To do that I almost never skipped a tournament.

After '73 I wasn't looking forward to '74. That was the first time I ever had that feeling. I just didn't want to put myself through it anymore. I didn't want to go for #1. It was hard to back away, but I just couldn't take the pressure anymore. With that in mind, I considered retiring.

I didn't retire, but when I went back in '74, something changed. When I'd find myself in contention, I'd shoot a horrible score. I didn't know why it was happening until a good friend pointed it out. He said, "You're intentionally backing away when you find yourself in contention. You find a way to shoot yourself out of it to take the pressure off."

It sounded crazy, but I thought about it and realized he was right. To fix that problem I needed a new mindset. I came to the conclusion that instead of trying to be the leading money winner and playing every week, I would take some time off, but still try to win when I played.

That was a huge realization. I won some tournaments that year, but I wasn't the leading money winner. I didn't put that pressure on myself anymore. This new mindset extended my career.

I remember when I won the Dinah Shore in '77. It catapulted me to #1 on the money list and I thought, "Oh dear, not again!" Within the next week or so we played at Forsgate C.C. in New Jersey. I always loved that course and again I won.

The next week I played terribly and missed the cut. It was because I was back in that syndrome again. Actually it was good that I missed it, because that night I was lying in bed and I couldn't move. I know it was psychological, but I actually couldn't move. I was supposed to go to dinner with some friends from New York, but I couldn't. I remember thinking that I couldn't tee it up the next day even if I wanted to.

Those are some of the things that players go through being #1. It takes its toll. Fortunately I recognized it and had people help me get through it.

I think it's good that players take time off. I know the sponsors aren't thrilled about it, but it extends your career. I'm sure that it extended mine.

The Hare and the Tortoise

I WAS A fast player and it complicated things when I played with slow players. Consequently, it wasn't a lot of fun for me to play with them. However, I'd rather play with them than behind them!

111

Maybe that's one place where the tour could have done a better job. Some players are too slow and it slows down the entire field. Perhaps part of it was that I was too fast, but somewhere there has to be a happy medium.

The pace of play on both tours can be unacceptable. If a round of golf takes over five hours, it just wears you out. It's hard to keep your concentration that long. It's also hard on the gallery and hard on the television audience. It's exhausting.

I enjoyed a round so much more when it was faster. There were times when I teed off early because I had a bad round the day before, but I still looked forward to it. At least I could play at my own pace. And with few exceptions, I played better.

An interesting thing about players that are notoriously slow is that they don't think they're slow. They absolutely don't think so. When they are talked to about speeding up, they look at you like, "What do you mean? I'm not slow." That's a tough nut to crack.

It's funny though, when they know they're on the clock, they speed up a lot. So somewhere deep down inside they must know they're not fast. Unfortunately, as soon as they're off the clock, they slow down again.

Knowing your game and having an idea which club and shot you're going to hit by the time you get to your ball really speeds things up. If the lie allowed it, I pretty much always knew the club and shot I was going to hit by the time I got to my ball.

One of the reasons for slow play might be that players chat so much walking down the fairway that they first start calculating the distance and other factors when they get to the ball. If they had an idea of what they're going to do before they got to the ball, maybe it would make the process quicker.

Some players stare and think and look. It just amazes me. I ask myself, "What are they trying to figure out? Maybe they're considering how the rotation of the earth is going to affect their shot?"

112

Sudden Death Playoffs

I USUALLY GOT beaten in sudden death playoffs. It had nothing to do with anything other than I just didn't like them. It became too personal.

It was just me and that other player. I didn't like that. It was unpleasant. I didn't want to beat up on them, and I didn't want them beating up on me.

Also, there was gamesmanship involved and I didn't like that either. Everything about it was distasteful. I wish I didn't feel that way about it, but I did. And nine times out of ten I came out on the short end of the stick.

I Never Choked

DURING MY CAREER, I definitely made some mistakes coming down the stretch, but I don't feel that I ever choked. If I had a lead, most of the time I was able to bring it home.

There were times when I stumbled and other times when someone would shoot a 64 or something and flat-out beat me. But I didn't get scared or nervous to the point that I couldn't perform.

Probably the main reason that I didn't choke was that I learned to enjoy the feeling of nervousness. It was exciting to me. The combination of being in the hunt and getting a little jumpy made it thrilling.

Part of the ride was putting myself on the line. I liked that. I knew that I had the opportunity to test myself and my ability.

While it was happening I was thinking, "Gosh, this is what it's all about."

I tried to put myself there every week. I never backed away from it and I was never afraid. There is a big difference between being nervous and being afraid. Afraid means thinking, "What if I mess up?" or "I can't do it." That must be a terrible feeling.

I was never afraid, so I never choked.

Would McDonald's Help Burger King?

IF MCDONALD'S HAD a downward trend in their business, would they feel comfortable asking Burger King for help? And if they did ask, would Burger King try to help them out?

Tour players are competitors who are scrapping for as much of the purse as they can muster. That being the case, isn't it interesting that they try to help each other out?

I went to Mickey several times for help over the course of my career. She would never volunteer information, but she also would never say "No." Or, "I don't want to talk about it." That never happened. It could have happened, but it never did.

I don't know of anyone who was ever refused when they asked for help. From the stories that I heard, nobody ever said "No" to anybody. It was always, "Oh, sure."

Occasionally a player would come over to me and we'd talk about a few things. I was thrilled when someone would ask me a question. I was glad to share what I knew. It was just great if I could help them.

It never crossed my mind to say "No" to anyone who asked me for advice. I considered it a compliment if they'd come to

114

me and say, "Would you help me out?" They must have respected me or what I had to say. "Do you see something? Would you help me?" Those words were music to my ears.

It was such a nice atmosphere on tour. It's a wonderful thing to be comfortable enough to be able to go up to someone and ask for help. I think it's the nature of the people who play the game.

Golf is such a hard game and we were more than willing to help out our competitors.

Fishing for Peace of Mind

I'VE SAID THAT golf was on my mind 100 percent of the time. That's actually not totally true because once in a while I had to take a break. Sometimes I had to shut my mind off.

If I found myself thinking about the swing too much, I'd go to a movie. I would do anything to break that cycle. Fishing was also something that I enjoyed doing that took my mind off of golf. At least it did to some degree.

In a way, fishing was pretty much like golf because it's just you and the fish. I really enjoyed fishing for that part of it. It's funny that there are a lot of golfers who are also fishermen.

There were times when I had to think about my game and times that I didn't. In the beginning I didn't know that. Later I realized it. Sometimes I had to shut it off by going on mental vacation and fishing for peace of mind.

Getting a Big Head

I REALLY DON'T know how this happened. I was horrified when I found out. It's not that I was conceited or talking about how great I was. This was what happened.

I had just come off a really good year in 1963. I won eight tournaments. I guess I started to read the newspaper clippings and I should have known better than to do that.

In 1964 I played well, but I just couldn't win. My first teacher, Hardy Loudermilk, came out to watch me and noticed something. He said, "You're getting a big head." I thought, "What! Me! That's impossible!" But I knew Hardy never would have said it if he didn't think it was true. I took a closer look and realized that Hardy was right.

Instead of grinding on each shot, I expected the ball to go where I wanted it to go because of who I was and how I played in the past. I thought, "This ball should be going in the hole or this ball should be going here or there." I was surprised when the ball didn't go where I wanted it to. It was almost as if I was saying to the ball, "Don't you know who I am?"

Guess what? The ball never heard of me! Anyhow, that was the bad attitude I developed. I played a practice round after I talked to Hardy and thought "Oh no, he's right."

I played in the pro-am (San Antonio Civitan) and I was able to have two days of practice before the tournament started. I won the tournament, but it was one of the hardest tournament wins in my career. I had gone through the whole year with this bad attitude and it became a habit I had to get rid of.

I was expecting good things to happen instead of grinding to make them happen. I got a big head and I didn't realize it. Thank goodness Hardy did. I never took winning for granted again. That was a great lesson.

Beware of an Injured Golfer

THERE'S A SAYING, "Beware of an injured golfer." Many times it's true. They feel so bad, they just have to play and survive. It's funny how that happens.

Actually, they might be hitting the ball better because they're swinging within themselves. Of course when they're feeling better and try to recreate that swing, it doesn't work.

But it is an interesting phenomenon that very often an injured or sick golfer can play their best golf.

The Importance of Being a Good Athlete

IT CERTAINLY HELPS to be a good athlete. Natural ability is always a plus, but of course it depends on what you do with it.

I've seen a lot of golfers who were good athletes with lots of natural talent who didn't have the desire to excel. They didn't dedicate themselves properly and never made it.

On the other side of the coin, I've seen golfers who were not as athletically inclined, but were hard workers, go on to have successful careers.

Then there were the good athletes who dedicated themselves and played great in practice rounds, but folded in competition.

Being a good athlete is part of it, but it's not all of it.

The best combination is a good athlete who is dedicated to improve both the physical and mental parts of his or her game.

A Fifty-Year-Old Mind at Twenty Years Old

I HAD TO be ready, willing, and able to accept advice in order to benefit from it. If I knew the things at twenty years old that I knew at fifty, I don't know how much it would have helped me, because I'm not sure I was ready. Was I mature enough at that stage in my life to understand and apply that knowledge? I doubt it.

There are a lot of things that people will tell you, but you have to believe it's correct. If you haven't had enough experience, you may not know if it's right or wrong. Also, you have to respect the person who's telling you.

Sometimes you have to experience things yourself and learn from those experiences, or at least realize that's a place you have to visit. It can be hard to learn when it's just somebody telling you what to do. Of course if they're correct, it would be nice to learn that easily. As they say, "A word to the wise is sufficient."

I'm sure there were lots of things that I knew at 50 that would have helped me at 20 if I could have accepted them. But I just don't know if I was ready. Sometimes you have to realize that you have a problem before you see a need to fix it.

For example, at twenty years old I might have thought that my shot selection was fine, even though a fifty-year-old Kathy would look at that decision and be amused.

You have to grow into it, be ready for it, and realize that there's a need.

Holding a Lead

IF I WAS in the lead with a few holes to go, I was very conservative about it.

I tell this story about the Nabisco Dinah Shore. It was Joanne Carner and I coming to the last hole and I had a 2-shot lead. Joanne was in the group ahead of me and I knew she would birdie the par-5, 18th hole. She was such a good competitor and she was playing so well that I decided that I needed a par to win.

On my drive, since there was water down the left side and there weren't that many trees on the right, I wanted to bail out to the right rough. I knew it wouldn't be that hard of a lay-up second shot from there.

I hit my push-fade block and it went where I wanted it to go. I wasn't going to lose it left. People watching must have thought, "Oh no, she hit it into the right rough." I just thought, "Yes!"

I knew the area over there was okay and I wasn't worried about it. I had a better chance hitting it there than putting pressure on myself and trying to hit it down the middle of the fairway with water down the left side.

As it turned out, my lie was fairly good and I hit a nice lay-up shot down the fairway. I hit my third shot on the green with a 9-iron and 2-putted for par. Carner birdied the hole and I won by a stroke.

I was in a similar situation in 1985. Amy Alcott, who was one group ahead of me, was playing very well. She birdied 18 and I had a 1-stroke lead as I stood on the 18th tee. If I could par the 18th I'd win.

It was a par 5 and there was trouble down the left side off the tee. On the right side was a fairway bunker, but I knew that it was flat and firm and wasn't a bad place to be. I bailed out over there and hit it in the bunker. I went on to hit a simple lay-up second shot from the bunker and hit my third shot five feet from the hole. I lagged up the birdie putt and tapped it in for a par and my final victory.

I tried to do whatever I could to hold on to a lead. I used course management by picking areas where I could bail out and hit shots that I was pretty sure would go there. I just wanted to get it in the house in one piece.

I didn't care if my game was pretty coming in, as long as I was looking pretty at the awards ceremony.

Celebrities

SPORTS CELEBRITIES LOVE to play golf and we got to play with many of these wonderful personalities. But we didn't only play with sports celebrities. We also played with businessmen and other nice people.

They all loved to play the game. Maybe they weren't the greatest players in the world, but they contributed to the charity and were hoping to have a fun day on the course. I've met a lot of great and wonderful people in this game.

But there's something special, and it's such a treat, to play golf with someone you've seen on TV, who you root for in sports or possibly who you admire.

Here are a few of the celebrities that I've met through golf:

JOE NAMATH

Broadway Joe was an 8 or 9 handicap and a good guy. He wasn't that much younger than me, but when we spoke he always said, "Yes ma'am." I thought, "Oh rats. Maybe I'm getting old or something. Or, at least that he thinks of me as being old." But he was really sweet and polite.

YOGI BERRA

I hadn't been on tour very long and I was a great fan of Yogi's, so it was a great thrill to play with him. The Yankees were in St. Petersburg, Florida, for spring training and the tour stop was close by. It was interesting that he batted lefty but played golf righty. Maybe that was one of his "Yogisms."

JOEY BISHOP

Joey Bishop was fun, but he almost broke my back. When we were introduced on the first tee, he ran over to me and leaned me back as if he was going to give me a big kiss. I guess he wasn't as strong as he thought he was and I almost fell backwards.

The gallery might have gotten a chuckle out of it, but to be honest, it wasn't that funny to me.

DINAH SHORE

Dinah was just delightful. After seeing a celebrity on TV, sometimes people will say, "She can't be that nice." Well, Dinah was that nice!

In the early '70s, it was the thing to lend a celebrity's name to a tournament. There was "The Hope," "The Crosby," and the "The Andy Williams." Colgate asked Dinah if she was interested in lending her name to an LPGA event. Even though her game was tennis, she agreed. In time she worked on her golf game and became a pretty good golfer.

Dinah was a very special person and it broke my heart when she died.

LAWRENCE WELK

When I played with Lawrence Welk, my stock went up big time in my grandmother's eyes. I played with him a couple of times and he had a nice smooth swing. He had a little loop but his rhythm was, "A one, and a two, and a . . ."

DON MEREDITH

Don was a former Dallas Cowboys quarterback and a wise-cracking commentator with Howard Cosell on "Monday Night Football." He was also a pretty good country singer.

He would serenade us walking down the fairway. I don't remember what he was singing but just out of nowhere he would break out into a song.

JOHNNY MATHIS

I was always a big fan of Johnny Mathis and played golf with him just recently. I had a great time with him.

It just shows you that if you continue to be involved in golf, you don't know who you might meet.

PETER FALK

Peter Falk might have been pretty loose as a detective on the TV series, "Columbo," but he was as tight as a board when he was swinging a golf club. I tried to get him to relax a little. I told him that he looked like a cement wall.

He was so mechanical. He was trying so hard, bless his heart. He hadn't been playing very long, but by the end of the round he did get better.

TOM SULLIVAN

Tom Sullivan was a singer and he was blind. When you play with someone with a handicap you just say to yourself, "Oh man, isn't this just great that they don't let their handicap stand in their way."

I played with several blind golfers in Japan and their attitude was just wonderful. They'd smile and be in great spirits the whole time. It's a beautiful thing to be around. Afterwards I'd think, "How could I ever feel sorry for myself?

BOB HOPE

Playing golf with Bob Hope was such a thrill. I hadn't been on tour very long and I was doing an exhibition with Wilson. We were in L.A. and the Wilson salesman knew about a golf event. He asked me if I would like to play in a foursome with Bob Hope. I thought, "Wow!"

We weren't playing all that well and with two holes left he said to me, "I'll bet you a dollar that I can out-drive you." I said "Okay," and went on to hit one of my best drives of the day and out-drove him. On the next hole he said, "Double or nothing." I won again.

When we got in everybody was grabbing him to take him off here and there. I didn't expect to get the two dollars, but later in the evening he came over and gave it to me. I asked him to sign them and gave them to my sister. I wish I knew where they are now.

That was just so much fun. I got to play with him again later in my career and I also met his wife Dolores. She was a terrific gal and a great supporter of the LPGA.

Bob was actually a very serious player. He might have had a few quips to say, but it wasn't a laugh a minute.

Bob Hope was as nice as a person could be.

I Was Addicted to Golf

DURING MY COMPETITIVE days I thought about golf 100 percent of the time. Actually that's not true. There were times when I'd dream about something I was working on in my swing, so I guess you could say that I thought about golf more than 100 percent of the time!

It never got to the point where I couldn't enjoy being with people, going out, going to a movie or to dinner. But it was pretty constant.

Still, it was something that I wanted to do. It was something that I needed to do. That's the beauty of this game. Golf was always on my mind because I was always trying to do something better.

It's probably like a drug. Thank goodness I've never been addicted to a drug, but this was probably as close as I could get. It stayed with me all the time. There's no doubt about it, it consumed me.

It was constant until the season ended, but even then I was pretty much captive to the game. I was addicted to golf.

Lucky me!

Caddies: When No Action Speaks Louder than Words

I NEVER WANTED caddies to pick my clubs for me because I was usually working the ball one way or the other and different flights went different distances. I knew how far the ball would go with different ball flights and with different clubs, so I didn't need the caddie's help in selecting the proper club to play.

For example, if I was hitting a draw with an iron it would go one club longer than a fade. That's why before the tournament started I always told the caddy, "Please let me pick my own club."

In general, a caddy holds the golf bag near the ball and, after the player selects a club, he takes the bag away. But I've had caddies who would keep the bag there after I pulled a club to let me know that he thought that I pulled the wrong one. That's not exactly what I'd call a confidence builder, but instead an example of "no action speaking louder than words."

I understood how they felt and, if I was a caddie and thought my player was going to hit the wrong club, I would probably have done the same thing. Of course I'd probably get fired, but I'm not sure that would have stopped me. I would have been a bad caddie for me!

One year at the Nabisco Dinah Shore, I had a caddie who really wanted to help. He had his own way of speaking loudly without words. His trick was to gather all of the clubs on one side of the bag except for one lonely club on the other side. Of course that was the club he wanted me to hit. Somehow I won that year.

It was important for me to take responsibility for my own decisions on the course. There were times when caddies went a little overboard and when they did, I told them, "You do a lot of good things. You clean the ball, keep the clubs clean, hold the pin, rake the traps, carry the bag, and keep out of the other players' way. You do all that and I'm very appreciative, but I don't need you for clubbing. For another player it might be important, but it isn't for me."

Other than a few instances, I always had fun with the caddies and I hope that they enjoyed being with me. I never had a regular caddie, though. That's not to say that it isn't important. I think that in today's day and age it's a good thing, but I still think that there needs to be a line drawn between the player and the caddy, and the caddy shouldn't cross it.

I say that because I've seen it get to the point where a caddy decides what club the player hits and gradually moves into making other decisions. When it gets to that point, the player is depending too much on the caddie and eventually loses confidence.

It's alright to discuss things with a caddie, but in the end it's always the player's choice. Make your words speak louder than a caddie's actions if they cross the line.

My Hair

I STYLED MY hair by putting it up and then sprayed it with hairspray until it was fairly stiff so it wouldn't move during my swing. I didn't want it to be a distraction. It would take quite a strong wind to shift it.

When I was Jack Nicklaus' honoree at his Memorial Tournament several years ago, Dottie Pepper made a remark about my hair at the presentation. She said, "We knew it was a two club wind if Whit's hair moved."

Honestly, that was the first time that I knew my hair was a topic of conversation. Judy Rankin once made the comment about gossip on the tour by saying, "I was always the last to know except for Kathy Whitworth." Well, I guess she was right.

Too bad I didn't know what they were saying about my hair when I was playing on the tour. If I did, on a breezy day I could have used a little more or a little less hairspray. I could have played a little "hairsmanship!"

My Favorite Dream

Some days I wouldn't be hitting the ball very well and I couldn't figure out why. Something was wrong, but what? I'd go to the range and try and try and try, but nothing worked.

I'd lie down in bed that night and think about my swing, but still nothing. I'd fall asleep and sometimes I'd have a dream about my golf swing. Then my dream would give me the answer! I'd think, "Yes! This is it!" I'd jump up out of bed and look at it in the mirror. It always looked great!

I loved those dreams. But don't ask me if it worked the next day.

The Hogan, Nicklaus, Palmer, Whitworth Grip

The "Centennial of Golf" dinner was held in 1988 at the Waldorf Astoria Hotel in New York City. It celebrated the first 100 years of golf in America. I was invited and was sitting between Jack Nicklaus and Arnold Palmer on the dais. One of the speakers was Ben Hogan.

For some reason he started talking about his grip. As he described the positions, the pressure points and the feel, I put my hands under the table trying to do what he was saying.

As I glanced down at my hands to see what the grip looked like, I noticed that Jack's hands were under the table doing the same thing. I found that amusing and got my curiosity going about Arnie. I looked over and sure enough, he was doing the same thing.

I got a real chuckle out of that and I still do.

Getting Awards

AWARDS ARE TERRIFIC, but some are more fun and meaningful than others. A lot depends on what it's for, and when it comes along. My most recent award was the PGA's "First Lady of Golf." It was a great evening and I was very flattered.

The "Patty Berg Award" was so touching because Patty was such a great role model for me. She was way up there when I went on tour and she presented me the award.

There were times that I didn't feel completely comfortable about getting an award because I didn't feel that I deserved it. I'd feel, "Oh gee, I didn't do anything for anyone except myself and I had a great time doing it. I don't deserve to be rewarded for that."

Sometimes a group will give an award to increase awareness for their charity. Most are for great causes, so I got past the embarrassment part of it. They're doing it to gain recognition for whatever they are trying to raise money for. They chose me as their honoree, but I take the acknowledgment with a grain of salt and try to have a good time with it.

Golf is My Life

GOLF WAS AND is everything to me. I started playing when I was 15 years old and I still play. I also teach as well as being involved in many golf activities. I'm 67 years old and I hope to continue being part of golf for the rest of my life. I know it will be part of me.

It's fun to think about when I first went on the tour and all of those experiences. I remember how nervous and scared I was, and the excitement of playing on the LPGA Tour. It was such a thrill to meet the players who I envied so much like Mickey Wright, Patty Berg, Louise Suggs, and Betsy Rawls.

It's interesting that the wins and losses are not as memorable as thinking about the people I've met.

How about that first day when we played golf instead of tennis? I knew right then when I was 15 years old that my passion and love was golf. I just can't imagine what I would have done or what would have happened if we played tennis that day and we didn't play golf.

Who would have dreamed golf would be the catalyst for so many things including meeting and playing with hundreds of celebrities including Bob Hope? And it's still happening. I recently played golf with one of my favorite singers of all time, Johnny Mathis.

Traveling all over the country and around the world was so exciting. It's been a heck of a ride and a most wonderful life.

My original sponsors gave me enough funding to play for three years and my parents took a lot of pressure off me by saying that if I didn't make it, it wasn't the end of the world. They said if things didn't work out that I could come home and do something else.

That took the world off my shoulders, but the question still remains, "What would I have done if I did have to go home? There weren't too many jobs available for women at that time. Mostly there were secretarial jobs and openings for school teachers. I liked the idea of being a cowgirl, but I'm not sure how I would have gotten into that.

I do know that I had to be outdoors. If someone ever wanted to torture me, all they'd have to do is to tell me that I couldn't go outside anymore. I feel free in the outdoors. That was one of the most beautiful things about golf. It allowed me to be outside all the time.

Golf was and is everything in my life. I don't know what else to say.

The Fabulous Four

WHEN I WENT on the LPGA Tour, there were four women who meant so much to me and my career. Their examples as both players and people were priceless. As my role models, I observed closely how they conducted themselves. It was always in a professional manner with high standards and integrity.

I never could have achieved what I did without the influence of these four fabulous women. They were Mickey Wright, Patty Berg, Louise Suggs and Betsy Rawls.

MICKEY WRIGHT

Mickey was just the greatest. She, by far, had the best swing on the tour. Ben Hogan himself once said that she had the best swing in all of golf.

Mickey was a perfectionist. She wanted to hit every shot dead, solid, perfect and she came closer to doing it than anybody.

She hit some shots that were just way out of my league. I remember nailing a drive and saying to myself, "Let's see you catch that one Mickey." When her drive flew past mine I just had to laugh. Well, at least I had the honors!

She was very gracious and had so much charisma. There was no doubt that she had the largest gallery, and not only because of her playing ability. It was her demeanor and how she handled herself.

Mickey was always working on her swing. She would try a few things and if it didn't work she would discard it. That in itself is a talent. She was able to decipher what would work for her and what wouldn't.

I like telling the story that in my first big year, 1963, I won eight tournaments but Mickey won thirteen.

Mickey was the best player I ever played with and she helped me so much in my career. She was basically the only person, except for Harvey, who I went to for help. She told me some things that turned my game around. I respected her and I knew that she wouldn't tell me anything that wasn't correct and true.

Mickey, I can't thank you enough.

BETSY RAWLS

Betsy had an incredible mind and was a great student of the game. In college she was a Phi Beta Kappa. She was also one of the nicest, humblest people you'd ever want to meet.

She and Mickey became really close friends and would talk about the swing a lot. I'd see them out there hitting balls together and talking back and forth. As the story goes, when Mickey was more concerned with hitting perfect shots than getting the ball in the hole, Betsy straightened her out.

Betsy knew what worked and what didn't work. She didn't have the greatest swing, but it was very effective. Her short game was probably her strongest point. She wasn't a long ball hitter, but she sure could get it around the golf course.

She had all the shots and never gave up. I played with her in Spokane, Washington, in my rookie year. There was a dogleg right that she cut off a little too much. It was rocky and her ball got a bad kick off a rock and ended up on the side of a mountain. She was able to manufacture some shot and get it in front of the green. She chipped up and made the putt for par. Meanwhile, I was in the fairway struggling to make par on the same hole.

It was just so much fun to watch her putt. That ball was always traveling at just the right speed and could go in from any side.

Betsy also had a sweet personality and wouldn't hurt a fly.

PATTY BERG

Patty was great to watch. She was an excellent ball striker, a great wedge player, and a fine putter. She was a shot-maker and a great competitor. She always kept the ball in play. The mistakes she made were minor. Patty was a complete player.

She played wonderful golf on some very tough golf courses. Mickey talked about Patty shooting a 64 on one of the toughest golf courses they played. From Mickey, that's pretty high praise.

She beat up on Babe Zaharias some. Babe was her dearest friend and had a very outgoing personality. Some of the girls didn't know how to take it. Babe would walk into the locker room and say, "Who's going to finish second this week?" Patty said to her, "You better be nice to these girls. Every star needs a chorus line!"

Patty's exhibitions for Wilson were something to see. What an entertainer! If she hadn't asked me to do the exhibitions and to learn all of those different shots, I never would have become the player that I did.

I owe so much to Patty Berg.

Louise had a different style of play. It reminded me a lot of Ben Hogan because every swing and every shot looked the same. Not that she wouldn't play other shots when she needed to, but all of her shots had the same flight.

I copied something that she did in her putting setup that helped me. While Louise was looking over a putt, she'd sort of lift her head and look at the line standing taller. I found that when I did that, it gave me another perspective.

Louise had high standards and was extremely honest. She expected people to be honest with her as well. If someone wasn't, she didn't have a lot of patience for them. I think that's the way it should be.

Louise was an outstanding player and person, and I always enjoyed playing with her.

Working on My Game These Days

I DON'T PLAY or practice nearly as often as I used to. When I know that I'll be playing a round of golf or making an appearance, I'll bring a club in my office to look at and feel my swing. After all these years, I know where the club should be and how it should feel coming through. I know what's correct for me.

So I'll swing in the office and maybe hit waffle balls in the yard. Waffle balls might not be as good as the real thing, but it allows me to take a full swing and to hit at something. At least the intent is there.

Life After the Tour

SINCE RETIRING MEANT shutting the door, I wanted to be really sure that I was ready to leave the tour. Everyone is different in their time frame and their reasons when they quit. I thought about it for several years and realized this was the time.

Mickey said, "You'll never find anything as exciting as playing on the tour." I knew she was right.

I shut that door, never looked back, and I never regretted it. I would have loved to be younger and still play on tour, but I knew that wasn't going to happen. When I quit the tour, I had no idea what I was going to do.

After retiring I went to the PGA Merchandise Show for the first time in forever. All the people in the golf industry were there and I wanted to let them know that I was available. I was still on the Wilson staff and as I was walking into their booth, Sam Snead and his agent were walking out. Sam introduced me to someone who was representing Don and Nancy Panoz. They were building The Legends Course at Chateau Elan in Georgia, north of Atlanta.

The theme of the golf course was legends. They had Gene Sarazen and Sam. They decided they would also like to have a lady legend and they selected me. They made a bronze statue of the three of us which stood outside the clubhouse.

One of the other things that I do is give speeches. Well, actually they're not speeches as much as telling stories about things that happened in my career.

It's something that I enjoy doing. Someone once gave me very good advice. They said, "Just tell about yourself and your experiences." I thought, "Okay, the subject of me is something that I know a lot about!" That freed me up from any inhibitions and it became fun for me and the audience.

Charity events are another venue where I make appearances doing clinics and playing.

When Wilson decided they wouldn't have any staff players, representatives from the golf club company Square Two asked if I would like to represent them. I signed a five-year contract. They made a nice line of clubs and put my name on them. I really enjoyed playing their equipment.

In terms of playing golf these days, I'll play two or three times a week for a few weeks and then not play for a couple of weeks. I still enjoy playing very much. I play at the Trophy Club in Trophy Club, Texas. They have been so wonderful to me.

Most of the golf I play is just social golf. During the round I spend most of the time trying to help people with their games. That's okay, they're good friends. But I miss those days when I was on the course competing.

Mom and Dad

MOM DIDN'T PLAY golf and wasn't a cheerleader type. Dad spent most of his time in our hardware store. But if golf was something that I wanted to do, Mom and Dad supported me in any way they could.

Aunt Nell was Mom's sister and I played golf with her. She took me to a lot of little tournaments and ladies events. I didn't know it at the time, but Aunt Nell and Mom talked to my first teacher, Hardy Loudermilk, about what I might need to continue to improve.

Mom always saved a little extra money to help me out, but it wasn't a matter of taking money away from the other kids. My two sisters, Carlynne and Evelynne, were already out of the house.

Mom and Dad always knew when I played badly, because I would come in the house and slam the front door. They left me alone, but at the same time they were so supportive and encouraging. If I had a good round, they'd say, "Great!" If I had a bad round, they'd say, "Good try!" They knew I was in my own little world and that I didn't need to be motivated.

My parents were more aware of my golf game than I knew. Without me knowing, Hardy went to Mom and suggested that I go see Harvey Penick. Hardy didn't ask me. He asked Mom.

Mom and Dad made that happen for me. Mom and I drove 500 miles to Austin and stayed in a hotel for three days. Mother would sit there during the lesson and take notes. I recently came across a paper sack with her notes in it. After I left, Hardy and Harvey would speak on the phone. Harvey would tell Hardy what I needed to work on and Hardy kept an eye on me.

To go on the tour, Dad and Hardy got together with a few businessmen and put together enough money for me to go out there for three years. When it was time to go, Mom and I took off in the family automobile. She stayed with me for the first month. It was so much better than being alone. Gosh, neither of us had been very far out of New Mexico. It was a grand experience.

She got very involved in the LPGA and the players. She would sit in the locker room and wait for the girls to come in. The players got to know her and they loved her. She'd sit around and listen to their stories and she'd be very encouraging to them. I got a big kick out of it and I know Mom enjoyed it too.

After playing poorly in my first ten tournaments, there was a two-week break and I drove home. I was feeling so badly about my game and I told Mom and Dad how I felt. I told them that I hated to waste their money. That's when Dad said something that changed my career. "You have backing for three years," he said. "If it doesn't work out within three years, just come home and do something else."

Knowing that freed me up. It made sense to me and it took off the pressure. My mindset was that I didn't have to do it today or tomorrow. I had three years. I felt that was a good gauge, and if I couldn't do it in three years, I should come home.

After the two-week break, I went back on tour and within the next few weeks I won my first check. I tied for last place with three other girls. The check was for $36 and I felt like I won the tournament. It was in Nashville, North Carolina, and was a major, major step for me.

I was fortunate that I went out on the tour when I did because I learned while I was out there. You can't do that today.

Mom and Dad were just great. They'd come to a few tournaments to watch me. Every year, for the first three or four years, Mom would come out with me the first part of the year and spend a few weeks. They were just terrific.

Setting the Record

WHEN I GOT close to records, the press was on it, so it was on my mind. But I must say that it was never a goal. I wasn't thinking that Mickey won 82 times and I wanted to win more tournaments that Mickey. It never crossed my mind to break Sam Snead's record of 86 wins.

Those were just numbers and weren't of primary importance to me. Winning was what it was all about. Every time I played I wanted to win, but the total number wasn't an issue.

When I got close to Mickey's record, the press asked me about it whenever I was in contention. They'd ask, "Will you win this week? How about next week? When will you do it?" I just thought, "Oh Gosh!"

It got harder and harder to win.

I tied Mickey's record and then came the questions about breaking it. Then after that I thought, "Okay, that's over with." But then they started with Sam. They were going down that road again. It was a relief when I finally broke the record.

But to me, 88 was just a number. The fun part was trying to win every time that I played.

Kathy's Career
Playing Record

MAJOR TITLES (5)

1965: Titleholders Championship

1966: Titleholders Championship

1967: LPGA Championship, Western Open

1971: LPGA Championship

1975: LPGA Championship

LPGA TOUR CHAMPIONSHIPS (88)

1962: (2) Kelly Girls Open, Phoenix Thunderbird Open

1963: (8) Carvel Ladies Open, Wolverine Open, Milwaukee Jaycee Open, Ogden Ladies' Open, Spokane Women's Open, Hillside Open, San Antonio Civitan Open, Mary Mills Mississippi Gulf Coast Invitational

1964: (1) San Antonio Civitan Open

1965: (8) St. Petersburg Open, Shreveport Kiwanis Invitational, Blue Grass Invitational, Lady Carling Midwest Open, Yankee Open, Buckeye Savings Invitational, Mickey Wright Invitational, Titleholders Championship

1966: (9) Tall City Open, Clayton Federal Invitational, Milwaukee Jaycee Open, Supertest Ladies Open, Lady Carling Open (Sutton), Lady Carling Open (Baltimore), Las Cruces Ladies Open, Amarillo Ladies' Open, Titleholders Championship

1967: (8) Venice Ladies Open, Raleigh Ladies Invitational, St. Louis Women's Invitational, Lady Carling Open (Columbus), Ladies' Los Angeles Open, Alamo Ladies' Open, LPGA Championship, Women's Western Open

1968: (10) St. Petersburg Orange Blossom Open, Dallas Civitan Open, Lady Carling Open, Gino Paoli Open, Holiday Inn Classic, Kings River Open, River Plantation Invitational, Canyon Ladies Classic, Pensacola Ladies' Invitational, Louise Suggs Invitational

1969: (7) Orange Blossom Open, Port Charlotte Invitational, Port Malabar Invitational, Lady Carling Open, Patty Berg Classic, Wendell-West Open, River Plantation Women's Open

1970: (2) Orange Blossom Classic, Quality Chek'd Classic

1971: (4) Raleigh Golf Classic, Suzuki Golf Internationale, Lady Carling Open, LPGA Championship

1972: (5) Alamo Ladies Open, Raleigh Golf Classic, Knoxville Ladies Classic, Southgate Ladies Open, Portland Ladies Classic

1973: (7) Naples-Lely Classic, S&H Green Stamp Classic, Dallas Civitan Open, Southgate Ladies Open, Portland Ladies Open, Waco Tribune Herald Ladies Classic, Lady Errol Classic

1974: (1) Orange Blossom Classic

1975: (2) Southgate Open, LPGA Championship

1976: (2) Bent Tree Classic, Patty Berg Classic

1977: (3) Colgate-Dinah Shore Winner's Circle, American Defender Classic, LPGA Coca-Cola Classic

1978: (1) National Jewish Hospital Open

1981: (1) The Coca-Cola Classic

1982: (2) CPC Women's International, Lady Michelob

1983: (1) Women's Kemper Open

1984: (3) Rochester International, SAFECO Classic, Smirnoff Ladies Irish Open

1985: (1) United Virginia Bank Classic

UNOFFICIAL TITLES

1968: Shell's World Series

1971: LPGA Four-Ball Championship (with Judy Kimball Simon)

1975: Colgate Triple Crown

1978: PING Classic (with Donna Caponi)

1980: Portland PING Team Championship (with Donna Caponi)

1981: Portland PING Team Championship (with Donna Caponi)

AMATEUR TITLES

1957: New Mexico State Amateur

1958: New Mexico State Amateur

OTHER ACCOMPLISHMENTS

Vare Trophy: (7): 1965, 1966, 1967, 1969, 1970, 1971, 1972 (most in LPGA history).

LPGA Player of the Year: (7): 1966, 1967, 1968, 1969, 1971, 1972, 1973

LPGA Tour's Leading Money Winner: (8) 1965–68, 1970–73

Associated Press Athlete of the Year: 1965 and 1967
Named "Golfer of the Decade" by *GOLF* magazine for the years 1968–77